INSIDERS' GUIDE®

KID'S GUIDES SERIES

The Kid's Guide to New York City

**Eileen Ogintz
with Reggie Yemma**

D1082039

INSIDERS' GUIDE®

GUILFORD, CONNECTICUT
AN IMPRINT OF THE GLOBE PEQUOT PRESS

About the Authors

Eileen Ogintz writes the nationally syndicated column "Taking the Kids," which appears in newspapers all over the country as well as on the Web. Reggie Yemma, Eileen's daughter, grew up just outside New York City and now attends college in Colorado. Reggie has helped her mom report on places that would be fun for kids since she was in elementary school.

INSIDERS' GUIDE®

Copyright © 2004 by Eileen Ogintz

Text design: Eileen Hine
Map design: Stefanie Ward
Photo credits: pp. i, 5, 6, 9 11, 22, 23, 25, 32, 33, 35, 43, 45, 50, 55, 57, 58, 69, 70, 76, 77, 82, 85, 87, 92, 96, 100, 105, 107 © Rubberball Productions; pp. 8, 15, 21, 39, 95, 108, 117 © Photodisc.

ISSN 1549-4276
ISBN 0-7627-3078-1

Manufactured in the United States of America
First Edition/First Printing

Contents

Acknowledgments

We want to thank all of the people who work and live in New York City who gave freely of their time because they want visiting kids to love New York as much as they and their kids do. In particular, the children who attend P.S. 6 in Manhattan, especially Lisa Schwartzburg's fourth grade class, and all of the educators at city museums, Central Park, and the city's historic sites. We also want to thank NYC & Company's Arleen Kropf, who never failed to answer a question, and Toys "R" Us in Times Square for allowing us to talk to kids while they were shopping. Thanks to Carrie Simmons, Stephen Bryant, and Janelle Nanos, all NYU journalism graduate students, for helping with the research. Most important, thanks to our favorite group of travelers: Andy, Matt, and Melanie.

The prices and rates listed in this guidebook were confirmed at press time. We recommend, however, that you call establishments before traveling to obtain current information.

CHAPTER 1

Welcome to the Big Apple!

Get ready to take a big bite out of the Big Apple!

New York City is so big that whatever you like—baseball or basketball, theater or art museums, dinosaurs or lions, playgrounds or stores, Chinese food or pizza—you'll find it here. And you're sure to find some things you never expected, too. That's why New York is always tops on kids' lists of places they want to visit.

Millions of parents and kids call New York City home. Many of them have come from around the world to live here. You've probably never seen so many different kinds of people speaking so many languages. The experts say 160 different languages can be heard in New York City, everything from Arabic to Spanish to Chinese. How many do you recognize?

New Yorkers may seem like they're in a hurry, but they are really nice. New Yorkers love their city and they want you to love it, too. Especially since that sad day when the World Trade Center towers fell on September 11, 2001, it seems everyone here has been going out of their way to be nice to visitors.

Check out all the big buildings. This is one place you won't get bored. In fact there's so much to do it's impossible to do it all, no matter how long you stay.

No matter what the people here wear or what language they speak, they're all still New Yorkers. The Algonquin Indians and other tribes were the first New Yorkers; they were living here

New York is a great place to people-watch. Write down or draw the weirdest outfit you've seen today . . .

_____

_____

_____

_____

_____

when explorer Henry Hudson showed up in 1609. He was actually looking for a passageway from England to the Orient when he stumbled into New York harbor. Fifteen years later, the Dutch settled here and named it New Amsterdam. But by 1674, the English were in charge and they renamed the busy settlement New York after James, Duke of York.

New York was always a happening place—especially during the American Revolution. Did you know New York City was the first capital of the United States? George Washington was sworn in as the first president here!

Where do you want to go first? This book will help you have the most fun, whatever you want to see. We've asked New York

Web Sites

www.nycvisit.com is the Web site where you'll find everything from maps, to what's happening when, to hotel deals for visiting New York City.

www.nyc.gov is the city's official Web site for everything you want to know about the mayor's office and city government. You can also find a subway map here, an online store that sells New York souvenirs, historic photos, and more.

City kids to help too. You'll see their ideas in every chapter.

Most important, leave lots of time to explore the city's neighborhoods, as well as museums! That's where you'll discover the real New York—from coffee shops and delis to playgrounds, toy stores, and firehouses. Stop by a firehouse when you're walking by; you might be able to get a tour—if the firefighters are not off fighting a fire! Ask if they have any T-shirts for sale with their engine or ladder company insignia. They make great souvenirs!

Taxis, Subways, and Buses

Got comfy shoes? The best way to get around New York City is on foot or on public transportation. Subways are the quickest way to travel, but because they're underground, you can't see the sights as you speed along. On a bus, at least, you can watch the city go by. Taxis are like having your own driver, but they're expensive. The trick to hailing a taxi is for your parents to stand next to the curb

and look for a yellow car with a light on top. Then put an arm up and wave. If it's available, the taxi will pull over to you. Once inside, don't forget to buckle your seatbelt and then ask the cabbie where he or she is from. Chances are it's some faraway country.

If you decide to go underground, you can map out your route on the big subway maps that are posted in every train station. Or you can ask at the token booth for a pocket map. This is also where you can buy a yellow Metro-Card that will let you and your family hop on and off the buses and subways all day. While you're waiting for the train, look at the tile walls along some of the platforms—they've often been decorated by local artists. You'll probably hear some music, too, played by musicians right in the subway stations—a New York tradition. Lots of kids take the subway to school and to their friends' houses.

A visiting kid says:

Buy an "I ♥ NY" sticker and put it on your bedroom door when you get home.

Melanie, 12, Connecticut

6

DID YOU KNOW?

Manhattan is an island just over 12 miles long and 2.5 miles wide, lying between the East and Hudson Rivers. It's shaped kind of like a fish. To get into or out of Manhattan, you've got to use either a bridge or a tunnel.

DID YOU KNOW?

In the 1920s, a New York sportswriter named John Fitzgerald overheard stable hands in New Orleans refer to New York City's racetracks as "the Big Apple." There are many apples on the trees of success, they said, but when you pick New York City, you pick the big apple. He named his newspaper column "Around the Big Apple." A decade later, jazz musicians started using "the Big Apple" to refer to New York City, especially Harlem, as the jazz capital of the world. The nickname has stuck ever since.

DID YOU KNOW?

New York City is made up of five different boroughs: Manhattan, Brooklyn, Queens, the Bronx, and Staten Island. The city needs at least four different area codes to handle all its telephone numbers.

DID YOU KNOW?

The pair of marble lions that stand outside the New York Public Library at Fifth Avenue and 42nd Street have been welcoming New Yorkers since the library opened in 1911. First they were called Leo Astor and Leo Lenox, after the founders of the New York Public Library, John Jacob Astor and James Lenox. But during the 1930s, Mayor Fiorello LaGuardia dubbed them Patience and Fortitude, for the qualities he thought New Yorkers needed to survive the Great Depression. And these names have stuck. Patience is on the south side of the steps and Fortitude to the north.

Lights, Cameras, Action

You might be able to be on TV—if you can get up early. Head to NBC's Studios at **Rockefeller Center** (between 49th and 50th Streets, off Fifth Avenue) in Midtown where crowds gather every day by 6:00 A.M. to be seen on the "Today Show." You can also head to **Times Square** (42nd Street and Broadway) where you might make it on the air at "Good Morning America." If you're lucky, the camera will catch you doing something funny or holding up a big sign, the more colorful the better.

A NYC kid says:

You can see the bridge and boats from my house. When it's dark outside. the bridge lights up too. It's super cool!

Jenna, 9, Manhattan

CHAPTER 2

East Side, West Side: Figuring Out NYC's Neighborhoods

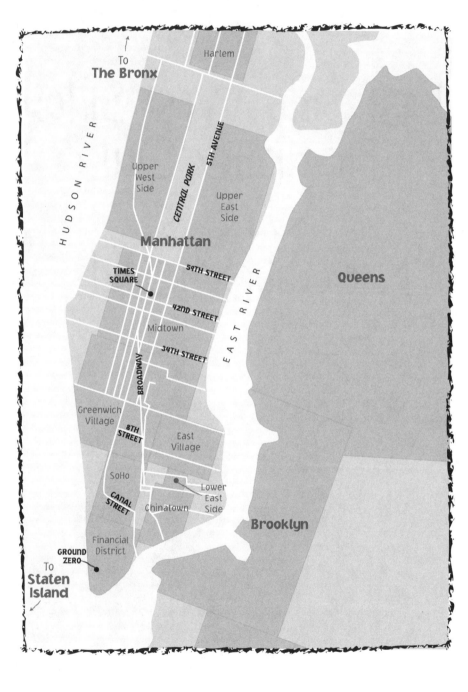

The best way to see how kids live in New York is to walk around the city's neighborhoods.

Manhattan is split by Fifth Avenue into the East Side and the West Side. You'll hear people talk about the Upper East Side and Upper West Side as if they were different countries! It's easy to understand New York if you think of it as a lot of little neighborhoods. Some neighborhoods have unusual names and if you know what they mean, you'll seem like a real New Yorker:

Harlem is north of 110th Street and has been home to New York's African-American community for a long time. There's also a large Dominican community here. Former President Clinton now has his offices in Harlem.

Midtown is just what it sounds like—the middle of town where there are lots of skyscrapers, restaurants, businesses, and stores.

Times Square at 42nd Street and Broadway is the heart of the theater district—and one of the liveliest tourist areas in the city—especially for kids.

SoHo is short for "*So*uth of *Ho*uston Street" (make sure you pronounce Houston like "HOW-STUN"—not like the city in Texas!). It's a neighborhood in lower Manhattan that has become one of the fanciest parts of Manhattan.

TriBeCa, on the Lower West Side, is short for *"Tri*angle *Be*low *Ca*nal" Street.

Chinatown and Little Italy are Lower Manhattan neighborhoods where Chinese and Italian immigrants settled and still live.

Greenwich Village started out as a seventeenth-century suburb, a "green village." Today it's full of people, cafes, clubs, and shops and is home to New York University.

The Lower East Side, once the center of Jewish life in New York, now is known for its stores and discount deals. This is one part of New York where you can still bargain!

Ground Zero is what they call the area of Lower Manhattan destroyed by terrorists on September 11, 2001. It's where the World Trade Center towers once stood. Plans are in the works for a memorial and new buildings. Ground was broken for construction on July 4, 2004.

Here's a tip from local kids: Explore places in one neighborhood at a time. That way your feet won't get nearly so tired.

Web Sites

www.timeoutnykids.com will tell you what's going on around the city for kids. Pick up their magazine, *TimeOut New York Kids*.

www.nycparks.org can tell you where to find playgrounds, basketball courts, in-line and ice-skating rinks, and more fun places around the city.

www.nycvisit.com has downloadable maps of the city. Click on "Visitors" and then "Maps and Neighborhoods," and you can explore some neighborhoods online before you visit.

Remember, there's a lot more to New York City than just Manhattan. The Bronx, Brooklyn, Queens, and Staten Island are all part of New York City too. A lot of kids live in each of these boroughs, and there's a lot to see in each place:

The Bronx is to the north of Manhattan and the only borough that is on mainland. In the 1800s rich New Yorkers lived here but now many of the neighborhoods are poor and in need of repair. A lot of families visiting New York take the subway to the Bronx to go to the Bronx Zoo, the New York Botanical Garden, or to see the Yankees play at Yankee Stadium.

Brooklyn is just to the south of Manhattan and is packed with people, trendy neighborhoods, immigrants from other countries, parks, and museums, like the Brooklyn Children's Museum, Prospect Park with its own zoo, and the Brooklyn Botanic Garden. There's also Coney Island, with its beach, amusement park, and minor league baseball team.

If you flew into New York, chances are you arrived in the New York City borough of **Queens**, at LaGuardia or John F. Kennedy international airports east of Manhattan. Temporarily, the Museum of Modern Art is here, while its Manhattan home is rebuilt. The Mets baseball team plays here at Shea Stadium. Queens is the biggest of the city's five boroughs and is home to many immigrants who have come to New York from India, Israel, Greece, Italy, Mexico, Korea, and other countries. If you went to school here, you'd hear lots of different languages every day.

Staten Island is south of Manhattan and seems more like a suburb to a lot of people. Those who live here commute to

Manhattan on the Staten Island Ferry. It's fun to take the twenty-minute ride just to see the skyline and the Statue of Liberty.

Let's Start Exploring!

Here we go. Got your camera handy?

You can start wherever you're staying. You might see some kids heading off to school, out shopping with their parents, or walking their dogs. Some kids spend all their time in their own neighborhoods, even though they live in such a big city. Ask some kids you see to point you to their favorite playground or pizza place in the neighborhood. They'll know—just like you would at home.

Most New York neighborhoods are only about 10 square blocks. And just like your neighborhood at home, they've got ice cream shops, pizza parlors, parks, schools, and lots of families and pets. For some kids, their apartment building is like your block at home. They play with kids in their building and make friends with the doorman, whose job it is to keep track of who goes in and out. On Halloween they trick-or-treat on the different floors of their building.

Even if you get to stroll through just one or two city neighborhoods, you'll realize New York is a lot more than skyscrapers, restaurants, and big stores: It's home to lots of families from all over the world.

In Manhattan, a lot of families live on the **Upper East Side** and the **Upper West Side.** How do you tell them apart? Everything east of Central Park is on the East Side. Everything west of the park is considered the West Side.

DID YOU KNOW?
There are more than 70,500 hotel rooms in New York. Where are you staying? What part of the city are you in?

DID YOU KNOW?
1.2 million kids go to New York City's Public Schools, more than in any other city.

DID YOU KNOW?
About 8 million people live in New York City's five boroughs, and about 1.5 million of them live on Manhattan Island, even though it is only 22 square miles.

DID YOU KNOW?
The name *Manhattan* comes from a Native American word that means "the place of hills."

DID YOU KNOW?
According to the U.S. government, New York City is now the safest big city in the country.

DID YOU KNOW?
You can walk or bike from Manhattan to Brooklyn across the Brooklyn Bridge. It's about a mile. The bridge took sixteen years to build in the late 1800s. It's such a pretty bridge, too, that New Yorkers love it. Bring your camera. The views of New York City are great!

DID YOU KNOW?
Some New Yorkers like to give FREE tours to visiting families and will tell you all their top picks in their favorite neighborhoods. Your family would need to make an appointment several weeks in advance, though. Call (212) 669–8159 or visit www.bigapplegreeter.org.

More than a third of the length of Manhattan is north of 110th Street. This includes the neighborhood known as **Harlem.** First settled in the 1600s by Dutch tobacco farmers, Harlem in the 1920s was the most famous black community in the country, maybe in the world. Many African Americans still live here and it's fast becoming a hot neighborhood again with new stores, restaurants, and attractions.

Think you want to be a star? The **Apollo Theater** on 125th Street in Harlem holds "amateur nights" to find new talent (212–531–5300; www.apollotheater.com). If you're a dancer, you might want to see a performance at the **Dance Theater of Harlem** (466 West 152nd Street; 212–690–2800; www.dancetheaterofharlem.com).

Farther south at 42nd Street is Times Square, which is filled with tons of cool things to see and do. Read all about it in the Times Square chapter!

A lot of kids who visit New York also like to head to neighborhoods south of 42nd Street, below Midtown, especially to eat, shop, and people-watch. Many families live downtown too.

Greenwich Village is bordered by Houston Street at the south end and 14th Street to the north and runs from Broadway west to the Hudson River. A lot of people just call it "The Village"—and it has lots of little stores, cafes, and parks. This is where New York University is, along with Parsons School of Design and the New School for Social Research. **Washington Square Park,** at the base of Fifth Avenue, is a great place to catch street performers —musicians, magicians, and break dancers. It is surrounded by

century-old houses and tree-lined streets where you'll meet all kinds of people, from kids on their way to school to teens with blue hair and grandparents who have lived here for decades.

At night, one block west of Washington Square Park, Sixth Avenue glitters like diamonds because of special material set into the road. On the opposite side of the campus, a few blocks east past Broadway, is **Cooper Square.** Right in the middle is a big sculpture that looks like a block balancing on its corner. Try to turn it and see what happens.

Head south of the Village for more shopping and eating in SoHo, Little Italy, Chinatown, and the Lower East Side, once the biggest Jewish community in the world.

SoHo runs between Sixth Avenue to the west and Lafayette Street to the east and goes down as far as Canal Street. Once a place where artists moved because they could get big loft spaces for little money, the neighborhood is now expensive, with lots of restaurants, trendy stores, and art galleries. If you like to make art, get messy at the **Children's Museum of the Arts** at 72 Spring Street (between Broadway and Lafayette; 212–941–9198; www.cmany.org). You might also want to stop in at the **New York City Fire Museum** (278 Spring Street; 212–691–1303; www.nycfire museum.org) while you're in the neighborhood to see how New York firefighters have always done their jobs. They also have old hand-pulled and horse-drawn engines they used in the old days.

Little Italy is east of Broadway, mostly around Mulberry Street. Around the second week of September, you can go hear music and eat all sorts of Italian goodies at the celebration of the Feast of San Gennaro. There's even a Ferris wheel you can ride that will take you high up above the streets.

Chinatown is just next door, below Canal Street, from Broadway to a street called the Bowery. Canal Street has lots of stores and shops where you can buy everything from watches to Chinese veggies. Chinatown is especially exciting during Chinese New Year, which is celebrated in late January or February. There's a big parade and performers dressed up as dragons or lions.

Older kids like the **Lower East Side,** east of the Bowery, because they can bargain with vendors on Orchard Street for better prices on everything from purses to T-shirts to sunglasses. More than one hundred years ago this neighborhood was home to many Jewish families who came from different countries. The streets were once teeming with peddlers selling their goods from pushcarts on the streets.

It can still be hard for all the kids who move to New York every year from other countries with their families—from Asia, Africa, India, the Caribbean Islands, and Central America, among other places. They may not speak English. They're not used to the weather, the food, or the crowds. Everything can seem different and strange. But New Yorkers are really glad they've come. They're part of what makes the city so great.

While you're downtown, make sure to visit the "Street of Ships" and travel back in time at **South Street Seaport.** Located on Fulton Street near the Brooklyn Bridge, it's one of New York's oldest—and now newest neighborhoods. For more than 300 years, the Seaport was one of the city's commercial centers, handling all the goods that came in and out of the port by ship—China clippers, Atlantic packets, Caribbean schooners, grain barges from the Midwest. But by the mid-twentieth century, the port's activity had moved elsewhere in the city. Almost a century passed before the city focused on South Street Seaport again. Now it has been redeveloped as a place to shop, eat, and learn a little history at the **South Street Seaport Museum** (207 Front Street; 212–748–8600; www.southstseaport.org).

You can visit one of the country's largest fleets of historic ships here and go on board one of them. Check to see if there's a special family activity for parents and kids when you're there. They have a lot of them on weekends. You might see woodcarvers at work on models and ship carvings at the **Maritime Crafts Center** on Pier 15. Or come watch a regatta or a concert in the summer. There's plenty of shopping too, especially at **Pier 17.** There has been a market here since 1822! And now there are more than one hundred stores and thirty-five restaurants.

New York Stories

You can visit Winnie-the-Pooh, Eeyore, Piglet, Kanga, and Tigger—the original stuffed animals that inspired the writer A. A. Milne—in the **Central Children's Room at the Donnell Library Center** (20 West 53rd Street; 212–621–0618), where you'll also find thousands of kids' books in many different languages. The Mid-**Manhattan Library** at 5th Avenue and 40th Street (www.nypl .org) is huge! However, there are public libraries all over the city

and in them—and at bookstores—you'll find many stories that take place in New York. Do you have a favorite? Here are some that New York's librarians think are the best:

- *The Adventures of Taxi Dog,* by Debra and Sal Barracca, tells the story of a stray dog that is taken in by a kind taxi driver.

- *Eloise,* by Kay Thompson, is the story of a six-year-old who grows up in the Plaza Hotel.

- *The House on East 88th Street,* by Bernard Waber, is about a New York family who finds a crocodile named Lyle in their bathtub!

- *The Cricket in Times Square,* by George Selden, follows the adventures of a cricket who ends up in the subway in Times Square.

- *Stuart Little,* by E. B. White, is the story of a mouse who lives with a family near Central Park. Did you see the movie?

- *All of a Kind Family,* by Sydney Taylor, gives a glimpse into what it was like for an immigrant family at the turn of the century.

- *Harriet the Spy,* by Louise Fitzhugh, follows the adventures of a sixth grader who lives in Manhattan.

- *From the Mixed-Up Files of Mrs. Basil E. Frankweiler,* by E. L. Konigsburg, tells the story of two Connecticut kids who camp out in the Metropolitan Museum and solve a mystery while they're there.

What's your favorite book set in New York?

Movies Everywhere!

Lots of movies and TV shows are set in New York City too, and many are filmed here. Just a few of them include

Spider-Man
Superman
Batman
Home Alone 2
Miracle on 34th Street
Ghostbusters
Stepmom
Stuart Little
Sesame Street
Reading Rainbow

How many others can you name?

CHAPTER 3

Times Square

MUSICAL

ADMIT ONE

ADMIT ONE

Quick. Think of a place in New York City where you can see your favorite music star, hear a gigantic dinosaur roar, or catch the latest news.

Stumped? Head directly to **Times Square.** At 42nd Street and Broadway, this is one of the easiest places in New York to reach by public transport as so many bus and subway lines stop here.

New York City kids like to come here because there's so much to do and see in just a few blocks. When your parents were kids, this part of town was so run down that families didn't like to walk around here much. The city has worked hard to clean up and rebuild Times Square in the last fifteen years, and now it's usually the first place kids like to come when they visit New York! A lot of people say it's like a city theme park with cool restaurants, big stores, theaters, and even the world's largest TV screen. There are 12,500 hotel rooms here—one fifth of all the rooms in the city—and more than 250 restaurants.

Check out all the giant signs! Some are huge advertisements, but you can also read the latest news lit up on a moving stripe at One Times Square. And since the late nineteenth century, this has been the center of the country's theater world. You can go to a Broadway show or a movie. You can join the crowd outside the **MTV Studios.** And you can buy souvenirs from the street vendors or in one of the dozens of stores that line the streets.

MTV

A good place to spot celebrities is at MTV's studios during the show "Total Request Live" (TRL), every weekday at 5:00 P.M. You can't miss it, on Broadway between 44th and 45th Streets. Just look for the crowd of kids outside. You might get on TV too, if the camera crews are there to get "teen-on-the-street" reactions. Which music star did you see? For more information check out www.mtv.com.

Check out **Madame Tussaud's New York Wax Museum** (234 West 42nd Street; 800–246–8872; www.nycwax.com), where you can "meet" The Hulk, Jennifer Lopez, or Michael Jordan—along with nearly 200 of their friends. Just one thing—they're all made of wax. It's not easy to pose for a wax portrait. Madame Tussaud's sculptors have to take lots of pictures and more than 250 measurements of each body. The sculptor models a clay portrait, and then the clay is molded in plaster. From that mold, the body is cast in fiberglass and the head from wax. Each pair of eyes is made individually—with hand-painted eyeballs to match the real ones. Hair color is perfectly matched to a sample given by the celebrity and each strand is inserted one by one.

The same goes with teeth. It takes five weeks just to make a head—six months to create the portrait. And every day, two teams inspect each figure to see if they need any "help" before the museum opens. They regularly get their hair washed and their makeup touched up! The celebrities often donate their own clothes and shoes so they'll look more real. Got your camera? You can pose for a picture with your favorite star. They look so real your friends might be fooled. Tip: If you whisper in J-Lo's ear, she blushes!

While you're on 42nd Street, peek inside Disney's **New Amsterdam Theater** (www.disneygo.com/disneytheatrical/newamsterdam) a few steps west of Times Square. It's the city's oldest Broadway theater, having opened in 1903, before a lot of your grandparents were born! And it's been completely restored. This is where *The Lion King* opened on Broadway and is still playing

to huge crowds. There's a big Disney store right on the same street.

You can also shop till you drop at **Toys "R" Us** (Seventh Avenue and West 44th Street), the biggest Toys "R" Us anywhere. Here's where you can see the giant *T-Rex* dinosaur, visit a three-story Barbie house, ride the indoor Ferris wheel, or try out the latest video games, ready and waiting.

New York kids also love the **Virgin Megastore** (Seventh Avenue and West 45th Street), which sells CDs, movies, posters, video games, and more. Another favorite stop is the **ESPN Zone** (42nd Street and Broadway; 212–921–3776), where you can eat, watch sports on giant-screen TVs, and play games. And you can visit all the little shops and street vendors selling "I♥NY" T-shirts, NYPD and NYFD hats, and statues and key chains of the Statue

New Victory Theater

This New York theater is devoted to parents and kids, with productions and performances all year long that are especially geared for families. It's located in a cool, restored building on 42nd Street just west of Broadway (212–239–6200). If you're eleven or older, their JVT (Junior Vic Teens) program has special events, such as appearances by cast members after performances. Check the Web site at www.newvictory.org to see if the theater is hosting any special activities while you're in town.

of Liberty. What souvenir will you want to take home?

Lots of families like to see a play when they're in New York City. You might get to go to one of the big Broadway the- aters, or even see what is called an Off Broadway play. That means it's a smaller, less glitzy production, shown someplace other than the big Broadway theaters. Tickets usually are cheaper too. Would you like to be an actor? Sometimes kids have parts in Broadway productions. They still have to go to school and do their homework, maybe in between their scenes. Sometimes they'll even move to New York City with their mom or dad temporarily to appear in a play. When they graduate from school, a lot of young people come to New York to audition for roles on Broadway. Many also work in restaurants as waiters or waitresses. Next time you're out at a restaurant, ask your server if he or she is an actor!

Make sure to eat something before you head to the theater. Otherwise, plays can seem awfully long (you can buy snacks in the theaters, but they're usually expensive).

A NYC kid says:

Make sure you've got a MetroCard to use on the subways and buses. You can get one at any subway station and then you just swipe it every time you ride.

Paris, 18, the Bronx

Hunger Pangs

New York is one place you can always find something to eat—and you don't have to go to a restaurant either. New York kids love hot dogs from the street vendors you'll see everywhere. (Try eating a hot dog New York–style with sauerkraut and mustard.) Big, soft,

hot pretzels also get thumbs up, or you can try roasted chestnuts or you can try roasted chestnuts or nuts. You'll also see vendors selling kabobs, ice cream, fruit, and Italian ices. Take your pick! And you can find any kind of food you want at the endless string of restaurants. New York kids like **Virgil's Real BBQ** (152 West 44th Street off Broadway; 212–921–9494) for ribs; **Carmine's** (200 West 44th Street; 212–221–3800) for Italian; **Ollie's Noodle Shop and Grill** (190 West 44th Street; 212–921–5988) for Chinese; **Ellen's Stardust Diner** (1650 Broadway at 51st Street; 212–956–5151); **Ben's Kosher Deli** (209 West 38th Street at Seventh Avenue; 212–398–2367) for a real New York pastrami sandwich; and **Cafe Un Deux Trois** (123 West 44th Street at Sixth Avenue; 212–354–4148) for a fun French experience, where you can write on the paper tablecloths and the fries are terrific. They don't call them french fries for nothing!

Despite all the activities, one of the best things to do in Times Square is just watch all the people. They are speaking so many different languages. Some are wearing really crazy outfits. Watch out! It seems like everyone's in a big hurry!

TKTS

Not many people like waiting in lines, but in New York, people don't mind waiting at the TKTS Booth at 47th Street and Broadway. That's because this is where you can get tickets for expensive seats for Broadway shows at half price. The catch: You can get

???

DID YOU KNOW?

The Toys "R" Us store in Times Square has the biggest indoor Ferris wheel anywhere—60 feet high—and it's the world's largest toy store!

DID YOU KNOW?

Broadway's nickname is "the Great White Way." Some people think that started when electric street lamps were installed here in the 1880s. Broadway is New York's longest street.

DID YOU KNOW?

More than 1.5 million people walk through Times Square every day. You can get here from anywhere in Manhattan and the outer boroughs by taking one of eleven different subway lines.

DID YOU KNOW?

There are more than 232 puppets in the Broadway production of *The Lion King* and twenty-five kinds of animals, birds, fish, and insects represented in the show. The giraffes are the tallest—18 feet high. The elephant is the longest—13 feet long. The tiniest is the trick mouse at the end of Scar's cane—5 inches. There are 143 people involved with the daily production of the show and only 53 are in the cast. The rest are musicians or people who work behind the scenes, including carpenters, electricians, sound technicians, and wardrobe experts.

DID YOU KNOW?

The **Times Square Visitors Center** (1560 Broadway, between 46th and 47th Streets; 212–869–5667: www.timessquarebid.org) is a great place to find out what's going on in the city when you visit. You can also pick up discount coupons, buy Broadway tickets, see what's up for kids, check your e-mail, and even send a Web postcard home to your friends.

Happy New Year

The New Year's Eve celebration in Times Square draws at least a half million people to the square and a billion more who watch on TV. The first New Year's ball dropped from the Times Square tower on December 31, 1907. The ball they use today is a geodesic sphere, 6 feet in diameter, which weighs approximately 1,070 pounds! It descends the 77-foot flagpole at One Times Square, formerly the New York Times Building, one minute before midnight, finishing its fall just as the new year begins. Take a picture of yourself in the middle of Times Square!

tickets only on the day of the performance and you've got to pay cash. TKTS has sold more than 43 million tickets since it opened in 1973. There's another TKTS booth at South Street Seaport (at the corner of Front and John Streets), and there you can also get matinee tickets for the next day. Both booths sell seats to the same shows. To find out more about Broadway shows, visit www.tdf.org/playbyplayonline/ and read *Play by Play*, an online magazine written by teens. You can also print out an application to apply for student discounts to shows.

Safety Smarts

New York is proud that crime is down. But you're still in a big city, so be careful! It's good to keep your wallet in an inside pocket.

Write down the name and address of where you're staying and keep those in your pocket too. If you don't know your mom's and dad's cell phone numbers by heart, write them down. If you get lost or separated from your family, don't panic! Just look for a police officer in uniform and explain what happened. If you're in a store, and don't see a police officer, tell a salesperson who is behind a counter and wearing a badge. The best advice is to stick close to your family and don't wander off by yourself.

Times Square Scavenger Hunt

Find:

__ Indoor Ferris wheel

__ Hot pretzel

__ Booth selling Broadway tickets

__ A tourist with a camera

__ The theater where *The Lion King* is playing

__ The latest news flash

__ An "I ♥ NY" T-shirt

CHAPTER 4

Must-See Sights

Where can you go in the middle of New York City and see five states? The **Empire State Building,** of course.

On a clear day from the Observatory on the eighty-sixth floor you can see New Jersey, Connecticut, Pennsylvania, Massachusetts, as well as New York. There's another observatory on the 102nd floor, but it's closed to the public now because the lines just became too long. New Yorkers look forward to seeing the colored lights on the Empire State Building from far away too—it's always green for St. Patrick's Day; red, white, and blue for Independence Day; and red and green for the Christmas season. But there are other times when they light up the building, too. Sometimes if a New York sports team is in a championship, they'll use the team colors to light the tower.

No wonder so many people make the Empire State Building, at 34th Street and Fifth Avenue (212–736–3100, www.esbnyc .com) one of their first must-see sites in New York. More than one hundred million people have visited the top of the building. Some people even get married here.

When you ride the elevator, you're going pretty fast, up to 1,200 feet a minute. Look around the elevator. You'll probably see parents and kids from lots of different countries.

In case you're wondering, the Empire State Building does get hit by lightning, about one hundred times a year. It was designed to serve as a lightning rod for the surrounding area. When light-

ning strikes the tip of the Empire State Building, it travels directly— and harmlessly—down a metal conduit into the ground.

Need some exercise? You can race up the 1,575 steps from the lobby to the eighty-sixth floor. Every year, there's a race to the top—and recent winners have run up all those stairs in under ten minutes.

A NYC kid says:

I ride my bike a lot, but it's smart to lock it up if you go inside. When kids came to visit me from out of town, they were always surprised my school had nine floors and an elevator.

Regan, 12, Manhattan

It's amazing that the Empire State Building was built in just one year, winning the race (with the Chrysler Building) to be the world's tallest building. It was designed to be eighty-six stories high, but they added 204 feet for radio and TV towers. The top of the building was actually built to serve as a docking port for dirigibles, the big hydrogen gas–filled airships that were famous in the 1930s—until the huge explosion of the *Hindenburg* brought an end to this. (Today's dirigibles—or blimps—are filled with the inert gas helium.)

Besides being famous for being so tall, the Empire State Building is a movie star. Remember *King Kong*? The finale of *Sleepless in Seattle* also took place here.

Take a good look around from the Observatory. What do you see?

Another way to see all of New York's buildings is to sail around them—on a **Circle Line Tour.** Some of these boat tours around Manhattan take three hours and will give you plenty of chances to take pictures of the Statue of Liberty, the skyline, the Brooklyn Bridge, and much more. The Circle Line leaves from Pier 83 at West 42nd Street at the Hudson River (212–563–3200; www.circleline.com). From May to October there's a much shorter high-speed trip on what's called *The Beast,* where you race by all the skyscrapers. You've got to be at least 40 inches tall to take the ride. Expect to get wet! The Beast leaves from both Pier 83 and Pier 16 at South Street Seaport. A similar boat trip, aboard the *Chelsea Screamer* leaves from 23rd Street, by Chelsea Piers (212–924–6262; http://chelseascreamer.com). There are also more leisurely boat trips: The schooner *Adirondack* (also from

DID YOU KNOW?

The Empire State Building has 10 million bricks and 200,000 cubic feet of limestone in its walls, floors, and ceilings. The building is 1,453 feet and 8 $^9/_{16}$ inches tall. It took just over one year to build what was for many years the world's tallest building.

DID YOU KNOW?

The official house for New York's mayor is called Gracie Mansion. It's on East End Avenue at 88th Street. But not all mayors live there. Mayor Michael Bloomberg chose to live in his own house instead. But there are lots of great parties and receptions at Gracie Mansion.

DID YOU KNOW?

The Radio City Rockettes have been kicking up their heels in their world-famous chorus lines at Radio City Music Hall for more than seventy years. The women may all look like they're the same height, but that's not the case. If you look closely, you can tell that the tallest women are at the center with the shortest at the ends. Besides starring in the Radio City Christmas Spectacular show, the Rockettes perform at the tree-lighting ceremony at Rockefeller Center and during the Macy's Thanksgiving Day Parade.

DID YOU KNOW?

You can avoid the lines at the Empire State Building if you buy your tickets ahead of time at www.esbnyc.org. If you go to www.citypass.com, you can buy one ticket that will get you into seven of the city's major attractions, including the Empire State Building. With these tickets you can save money and skip the line.

Chelsea Piers) takes guests on sunset sails of lower Manhattan (800–701–SAIL; www.sail-nyc.com), and New York Waterway boats cruise to historic spots along the Hudson, north of New York City (800–533–3779; www.nywaterway.com) from 40th Street and 12th Avenue.

Ready for some more cool buildings? Stop in at the **Chrysler Building** (405 Lexington Avenue, at 42nd Street). The old-fashioned, art deco lobby is worth seeing because there aren't many buildings like it. When Walter Chrysler built his skyscraper in 1930, he wanted the company's headquarters to make people think about his cars. The spire on top is supposed to look like a car radiator grill. There are decorations throughout that look like old-fashioned hood ornaments, wheels, and cars. Don't miss all the weird gargoyles on the building. There are even transportation scenes on the painted ceiling. How many scenes can you find?

Stop in at **Grand Central Terminal** while you're nearby (42nd Street at Park Avenue). It's been a landmark since 1913. Half a million commuters use this rail terminal every day. (It's called a "terminal," not a "station," because every train begins or ends its journey here). See the clock at the central information area? It has four faces. Then look at the blue ceiling upstairs. It's a painting of more than 2,500 stars. How

many constellations can you find? Tip: Little lights pinpoint them. A lot of kids like to stop in Grand Central to get a snack downstairs in the food court. Even if you aren't hungry, head down to the lower level toward the Oyster Bar. Right outside the restaurant where three passageways meet is **The Whispering Gallery.** Stand facing one corner and have a friend stand facing another. Whisper something into the wall. Your friend will hear it!

A visiting kid says:

The view from the top of the Empire State Building was my favorite thing in New York.

Phillip, 17, Sweden

On to the **United Nations Building**—which towers over the East River at First Avenue and East 46th Street (www.un.org). Your parents will definitely think it's a must-see. The U.N., of course, is the voluntary organization that countries around the world have joined to help keep peace, develop friendlier relations among different countries, and improve the lives of poor people. Maybe you've collected pennies for UNICEF at Halloween time. That is a United Nations effort. Certainly you've heard about U.N. peacekeeping troops being sent to different countries. Take a guided tour. You'll learn a lot about the work the delegates and staff do here, as well as about the building. Have you ever seen so many people from so many different countries in one building?

Are you visiting over the holidays? Anybody who visits New York over the holidays can't help but feel lucky. It is an especially exciting, festive time in the city. Walk down Fifth Avenue and look at all the store windows. They tell stories. Saks Fifth Avenue (at 50th Street) and Lord & Taylor (at 39th Street) are usually the best windows around. Go to **Radio City Music Hall** at Sixth Avenue between 50th and 51st Streets (www.radiocity.com) to see the *Christmas Spectacular* with the Rockettes. Or see *A Christmas Carol* at Madison Square Garden. Go ice-skating in **Rockefeller Center** or Central Park. During Hanukkah, you can see a massive Menorah at Fifth Avenue and 59th Street. And of course you want to see the giant Christmas tree in Rockefeller Center. You've

probably seen it on TV. The Rockefeller Center Christmas tree has been a tradition since 1931! A special team goes all around the East Coast looking for the perfect tree. They spotted the 2003 tree in Connecticut while flying in a helicopter. The Rockefeller Center tree starts in a farm or someone's backyard where it's been growing for years and years. When asked, families are usually happy to donate the tree, which is then carefully brought into the city with a police escort on a custom-made trailer. It takes at least fifteen people and a 280-ton crane to lift the tree into place. More than 26,000 lights on 5 miles of wire decorate the tree. The same star has been used on top for more than fifty years. It's 5 feet wide! After the holidays, the tree is ground into mulch and used in the city's parks.

Circus!

New York kids love the circus as much as kids everywhere. If you're visiting in late fall or winter, you might want to see the **Big Apple Circus** (www.bigapplecircus.org), a one-ring circus under a Big Top tent in a bright blue tent in Lincoln Center's Damrosch Park, at Broadway and 63rd Street. It has become a holiday tradition for New York families. There are acrobats, jugglers, dogs, clowns, flying trapeze artists, and more. The **Ringling Brothers and Barnum & Bailey Circus** comes to New York City in the spring. Check www.ringling .com to see if the circus will be here when you are. There's also an area on the Web site for kids. A tip: Go early and you might be able to talk to the animals.

Sightseeing Smarts

New York is so big and there's so much to do! You can't see it all. Here's how to have fun sightseeing:

1. Wear comfortable shoes.

2. Look at a map so you know where you're going. (You can get one at your hotel.)

A visiting kid says:

Always keep something to eat in your pocket.

Max, 7, Connecticut

3. Stash a disposable camera in your pocket and get your parents to take lots of funny pictures of you.

4. Alternate sites you want to see—like a museum or the Empire State Building—with some people-watching, time in the park, or time out for a meal. That way you won't get so tired!

5. When you get really tired, take a break. Go to a playground (there are more than 200 in the city!), get something to eat, or go back to the hotel and chill.

6. Alternate what you want to do and what your parents want to see. That way everybody gets to lead the pack—some of the time.

7. Buy postcards of all your favorite sites, jot down something about what you did there, and send it to yourself at home. The cards will be waiting when you get home!

CHAPTER 5

New York Museums That Kids Love

Ready to time travel? You can at New York museums, from prehistoric times to ancient Egypt to the future. You won't need a special vehicle, though. All you need to do is visit some of New York's amazing museums. It's impossible to see them all during one visit, of course, but there are some that are especially fun for kids.

A good place to start is the **Metropolitan Museum of Art** (1000 Fifth Avenue; 212–535–7710; www.metmuseum.org). It's so big that from end to end, the museum stretches 4 New York City blocks, a quarter of a mile. Just to give you an idea of how big it is, there are more than ninety bathrooms! Both the Met, as New Yorkers call it, and the **American Museum of Natural History** are on every family's top to-do list when they visit New York. That's why there are usually more visitors from out of town at the museums than New Yorkers. Approximately five million people visit the Met every year, making it the city's top tourist attraction. Nearly four million people visit the Natural History Museum every year. That's more people than live in most American cities!

A visiting kid says:

Take one of the guided tours of the Metropolitan Museum. It was really good.

Isabel, 14, Massachusetts

The Met has been around for more than 130 years. When you walk in the big front doors, you're entering one of the biggest and best art museums in the world. And even if you hate museums, this one can be fun as long as you know where to go. See if you can take one of the **Museum Highlights Tours** that are offered

several times a day. And don't forget to pick up some special family guides from the information desk. There are free kids' programs running all the time.

Of course you can't possibly see everything in one visit! And when you get tired, you can run and play all you want, because Central Park is just outside.

A lot of kids head for the ancient Egyptian **Temple of Dendur** first. In fact, it's one of the most popular exhibits in the entire museum. The Temple, built in the year 15 B.C., was taken apart in Egypt and transported by ship to New York. Engineers had to make detailed drawings so they would know how to put it back together exactly as it appeared on the banks of the Nile River. The temple had to be moved from Egypt because they were building a new dam that would have covered it in water. The government of Egypt was very happy the temple could be brought here and gave it to the United States as a present. The Met built an entire area to house the temple.

Kids also like to see the spooky mummies that are in galleries in the main building near the Temple of Dendur. Thirteen of the mummies contain real bodies from long ago, twelve of them adults and one child. We know that because museum experts

DID YOU KNOW?

There are 150 museums in New York City.

DID YOU KNOW?

The **American Museum of Natural History** has a special Web site just for kids with activities and fun facts about science and the exhibits you can see at the museum. Visit www.ology .amnh.org. While you're online, the **Metropolitan Museum of Art** has special brochures for families that you can download from its Web site (www.met museum.org).

DID YOU KNOW?

The **Brooklyn Children's Museum** (145 Brooklyn Avenue, 718–735–4400; www.brooklyn kids.org) was the first museum created just for kids. That was in 1899 and since then, 300 children's museums have opened around the world. Kids can work in a greenhouse, see plays and concerts in the summer at the rooftop theater, make a pizza, or sing a rap song. There's a huge "Totally Tots" area for very young kids. There is also the **Children's Museum of Manhattan** at 212 West 83rd Street (212–721–1234) with daily activities, including storytelling and arts and crafts. Find it on the Web at www .cmom.org.

DID YOU KNOW?

Many Museums are closed on Monday. Check before you go!

DID YOU KNOW?

The stretch of Fifth Avenue from 82nd Street at the Metropolitan Museum of Art to 104th Street, where you'll find **El Museo del Barrio** (www.elmuseo.org), has been officially named "Museum Mile".

DID YOU KNOW?

The largest framed painting in the Metropolitan Museum is "Washington Crossing the Delaware" by Emanuel Leutze. It is 12 feet 5 inches high, and 21 feet 3 inches wide.

did scans—similar to X-rays—of the mummies. They discovered that one of the mummified people probably died from some kind of accident because he had broken bones. There are thousands of objects here from Egypt besides the mummies. Take time to look at some of them—especially William the little blue Egyptian hippo. Can you find him?

Have you ever wanted to be a Knight in Shining Armor fighting battles with a big sword? You might not want to after you stop to see the Met's collection of **Arms and Armor.** Those suits were heavy! So were the weapons!

Girls especially like the **Costume Institute.** You can see the kinds of clothes people wore in different countries a long time ago by stopping in at the north end of the museum on the ground floor.

Of course you're not going to leave without seeing some paintings and sculptures. Take your pick—Impressionist art from France, sculptures from the United States, African masks, or Chinese porcelain. What part of the world do you want to visit today? Stop at any painting and imagine that you could step inside it. Where would you be?

The **Roof Garden** overlooking Central Park is a good place to take a break—and see giant sculptures that change every year.

Don't forget to stop at the **Children's Shop** on the second floor. You'll find more than 1,200 kids books as well as hundreds of toys, games, puzzles, and videos. No chance you'll leave without a souvenir!

If some of the things at the Met sound familiar, maybe you read about them in *From the Mixed-Up Files of Mrs. Basil E.*

Frankweiler by E. L. Konigsburg. Do you remember some of the other things Claudia and Jamie found on their adventure? Why don't you go on your own scavenger hunt and see if you can find them yourself?

Sure it's hard to pick. The Metropolitan Museum of Art has more than two million objects in its collections. But not everything is on view at once.

Think Dinosaurs. Lots of them. **The American Museum of Natural History** at Central Park West and 79th Street (212–769–5100; www.amnh.org) is home to one of the largest collections of vertebrate fossils—nearly one million in all!

This museum is the first one that many New York kids come to and they return again and again. The American Museum of Natural History has more than thirty million objects and specimens in twenty-five buildings and forty-five exhibition halls. More than 200 scientists work here.

Write down what you liked best in the museum.

_____

_____

_____

_____

If you want to see the dinosaurs first, head to the fourth floor. Did you know this museum has more dinosaur fossils than anywhere else in the world? Say "hi" to the *T. Rex, Apatosaurus, Stegosaurus,* and *Triceratops.* Stop at some of the computers to find out more about the dinos. Make sure to see the dinosaur nest.

Kids also like to see the huge dioramas in the mammal halls on the first and second floors that show you the animals in their native habitats—Alaskan brown bear, African elephants, water buffaloes from Asia.

Don't miss the giant totem poles in the Hall of Northwest Coast Indians on the first floor, the museum's oldest hall. It opened in 1896!

You'll probably also want to see the giant 94-foot model of a blue whale. She weighs 21,000 pounds! You can find her on the first floor in the newly renovated **Milstein Hall of Ocean Life.** When you find her, you'll be staring at the biggest model of the biggest creature that ever lived on Earth.

For ocean lovers, there are lots of other dioramas—of sea lions, dolphins, and flying fish, among others. You can find hands-on activities about the living oceans in the Kids and Families section of the museum Web site, www.amnh.org.

If you like rocks, you'll love the special halls where they display meteorites, gems, and minerals. There are more than 100,000 rocks here. Make sure to stop and look at the Star of India. It's the world's biggest blue star sapphire. The topaz crystal from Brazil weighs 596 pounds. Check out the Cape York Meteorite. It weighs 34 tons!

The **Hayden Planetarium** at the museum is really cool too. Did you know there are more than one hundred billion stars in our galaxy? You'll feel like you're in a spaceship at the Space Theater! It's all part of the big seven-floor **Rose Center for Earth and Space.** Follow the Cosmic Pathway through thirteen billion years, and don't miss the chance to see the latest news from space. You can also find rock samples and models from around the world.

The Museum's **Hall of Bio-diversity** is the place to go to see why we should all care about the environment and try to protect all different kinds of life. This is where you can visit a diorama of a rain forest from Central Africa. It's huge—90 feet long. Step inside to see what

happens to a rain forest when people don't take care of it. See all the leaves? They may look real, but each was made for the exhibit. How about all the bugs?

If you're visiting around the holidays, you'll love the Origami Holiday Tree decorated with Japanese paper ornaments in the lobby. Have you ever tried origami?

Make sure to allow plenty of time for the museum's hands-on Discovery Room on the first floor. Kids and their parents can get up close and personal with specimens, be part of a dinosaur "dig," solve puzzles, and even take apart and put together a big skeleton.

A lot of other New York museums are fun for kids too. Stop in at the **Lower East Side Tenement Museum** (90 Orchard Street, 212–431–0233; www.tenement.org) while you're shopping in the neighborhood. The museum is housed in an old tenement apartment building so you can see what it was like for immigrant families who lived and worked here a hundred years ago. Life was hard!

Back uptown, the **Museum of Television and Radio** (25 West 52nd Street; 212–621–6800; www.mtr.org) is one place where there's always something good on TV. Special family workshops are held so that kids can draw cartoons, create their own radio show, or find out more about their favorite TV shows—or the ones their parents loved when they were kids. You can even request a program and privately watch it at the museum. The museum has over 12,000 shows from more than eighty years of TV and radio.

Nearby, the **Museum of American Folk Art** (45 West 53rd Street; 212–265–1040; www.folkartmuseum.org) is the place to see quilts, old-fashioned dolls, toys, and moving sculptures. There are special weekend workshops for kids and their parents, as well as puppet shows and storytelling.

Don't skip the **Museum of Modern Art** just because it is temporarily housed in Queens. There are special family programs on Saturday and an Outdoor Family Film Festival in the summer. (Temporarily, the museum is at 33rd Street at Queens Boulevard in Long Island City, Queens, while a big expansion is underway in Manhattan. Call 212–708–9400 or visit www.moma.org for directions and details of the family programs.)

Closer to the Met, the **Guggenheim Museum** (Fifth Avenue at 89th Street; 212–423–3500; www.guggenheim.org) is one museum where it's fun to go in circles. The building was designed as a spiral by famed architect Frank Lloyd Wright, with the art hung on the walls alongside the curving ramp. Take the elevator to the top and look at the art as you head down. You may think some of these paintings are weird. A lot of people thought the building was weird too when it was built. They said it looked like a doughnut and a snail. What do you think it looks like?

Much farther uptown, on the West side, the **Cloisters** (Fort Tryon Park at 193rd Street) was put together from parts of buildings brought over from Europe, some more than 600 years old! Kids like to come to this branch of the Metropolitan Museum overlooking the Hudson River because they can play in the gardens and check out the brave knights and ferocious dragons on view. Don't miss the seven gigantic Unicorn Tapestries that were woven around the year 1500. How many different types of plants do you see in the tapestries? There are more than one

hundred. You can find out more about special family programs at the Cloisters by going to www.metmuseum.org and clicking on Family Programs and then the Cloisters. For recorded information call (212) 923–3700.

Following the river back down Manhattan you'll come across the huge aircraft carrier *Intrepid*—it's 900 feet long! This World War II fighting ship is permanently anchored with the submarine *Growler* and the destroyer *Edson* at the **Intrepid Sea-Air-Space Museum** (Pier 86 at Twelfth Avenue and 46th Street; 212–245–0072; www.intrepidmuseum.org). The USS *Intrepid* was launched in 1943 and sailed around the world for more than thirty years. You can see more than thirty aircraft, from very old fighters to modern jets, on the flight deck. You can also climb inside a replica of a Revolutionary War submarine or a fighter plane cockpit.

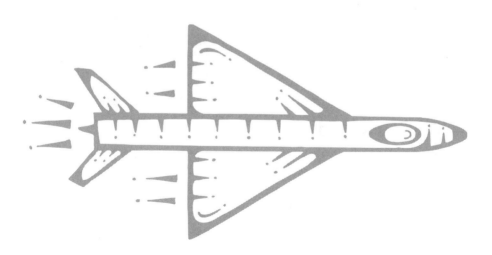

Check off what you saw at the American Museum of Natural History:

— *T-Rex*

— A dinosaur nest

— A brown bear

— A Native American canoe

— A totem pole

— The Star of India

— The Cape York Meteorite, the largest meteorite in the world

— The Discovery Room

— A rain forest

— An insect

— The Hayden Sphere

— The planets

— A butterfly

Museum Smarts

Museums can be lots of fun or very boring. To guarantee a good time:

• Go after you've had a snack. Don't go into a museum when you're tired and hungry.

• Wear comfortable shoes.

- Look on the museum Web site or ask when you arrive to see if there are special family activities that day or if there's a special area of the museum just for kids.

- Some museums are too big to see in a few hours, so zero in on a few exhibits you want to see. Don't worry about not seeing everything.

- Get some postcards at the gift shop when you arrive and have a contest to see how many "treasures" you can find. The Metropolitan Museum sells 1.4 million postcards a year!

- See some exhibits your parents (or siblings) want to see, and they'll be more willing to spend time in the areas that interest you the most.

- Leave time at the end for the gift shop. Museums usually have cool stuff for kids and in some cases, they even have special kids' shops.

CHAPTER 6

Parks and Zoos

Enough museums!

Let's have some fun in the sun . . . or the snow. It doesn't matter. **Central Park** is the place New York kids go to play, and you can too.

There's plenty of room for sure. Central Park stretches for 50 city blocks between the Upper East and West Sides—843 acres smack in the middle of Manhattan, from 59th Street to 110th Street and from Fifth Avenue to Central Park West.

It's been here for 150 years, since the city paid $5.5 million for the chunk of land that back then was virtually a dump. Today some New Yorkers pay that much for apartments just to have a view of the park. Maybe you'll want to take a horse-drawn carriage ride. You'll see them lining up just outside the park. Before you go to the park, check out the Just for Kids area on www.centralparknyc.org. Take a virtual kids' tour and find out more about the family programs that the Central Park has to offer.

Web Sites

www.CityParksFoundation.org is the Web site for a group that creates free kids' programs in New York's parks.

www.nycgovparks.org is the Web site for all New York City parks and recreation.

When you get to the park, stop in at what's called **The Dairy** (it's at 65th Street on the east side of the park). In the 1870s city children could get fresh milk here. Now the Victorian building is the Park Visitor Center and Gift Shop, where you can pick up a map and find out what's happening in the park the day you're there.

Nearby, you'll find the **Wollman Rink** on the east side between 62nd and 63rd Streets, where a lot of kids like to ice-skate in the winter—4,000 people skate here every day—and you can roller-skate when it's warm. You can rent skates. From May through September, Wollman Rink is transformed into a family amusement park featuring rides, games, and entertainment for the entire family.

Take your pick of other sports. You can in-line skate; ride horses; play tenni,; basketball, or soccer; sail model boats; even play chess in Central Park—and you can borrow or rent what you need to do it:

- *Rent bicycles,* even two-seater tandems, at the Loeb Boathouse parking lot at East 74th Street, daily from March through October.

- *Reserve a horse* from Claremont Stables, located at 175 West 89th Street, the only remaining working stable in Manhattan. Call Claremont at (212) 724–5100 for reservations.

- *Borrow a basketball* and play at the North Meadow Recreation Center, in the middle of the park at 97th Street.

- *Test yourself*–run around the Reservoir. It is 1.6 miles around.

- *Fish* at the Harlem Meer, stocked with a wide variety of fish, and located at the northeast corner of the Park. You can borrow a bamboo fishing pole and get some free bait (if you have a picture ID) at the Charles A. Dana Center, located on the north shore of the Harlem Meer at 110th Street between Lenox and Fifth Avenues.

- If you're older than eight, you can *rock climb* at the North Meadow Recreation Center, in the middle of the park at 97th Street.

- *Rent a rowboat* at the Loeb Boathouse (between April and October, East Side between 74th and 75th Streets) to take out on Central Park's twenty-two-acre lake.

- *Play chess or checkers* at the special tables inside the park at 65th Street just west of the Dairy. You can borrow chess or checker pieces.

- *Sail your own model sailboat* at the Conservatory Water, which is a small lake on the east side between 72nd and 75th Streets. (You can also call Central Park Sailboats at 917–796–1382 for information on model boat sales and rentals.)

Or you can snooze under a tree, climb some rocks, play Frisbee, or just chase your sister.

In the middle of the park at West 72nd Street, you'll pass **Strawberry Fields.** It's one of the park's most visited spots and was named to honor former Beatle John Lennon, who lived (and died) nearby at the Dakota (One West 72nd Street). He could see

this spot from his apartment building. Now it's an international peace garden with plants from every country in the world. Look for the mosaic in the pathway. It's inscribed with the word IMAGINE for one of Lennon's songs.

A lot of kids also like to hang out in the **Sheep Meadow** on the southwestern side of the park just north of 65th Street. (Yes, there were sheep here in the park's first years.) There's also a famous restaurant near here, **Tavern on the Green** (67th Street and Central Park West; 212–873–3200). Kids love to come here for special occasions because the dining rooms are so much fun with big mirrors, chandeliers, and murals. The restaurant gets all dressed up for the holidays with a life-size topiary gorilla and a horse.

Cross a bridge yet? There are thirty-six bridges in the park—no two of them alike—and 58 miles of paths to walk, skate, run, ride horses, or bike.

Don't miss the **Carousel.** (It's in the middle of the park at 65th Street.) The old-fashioned carousel is one of the largest in the United States, with fifty-eight hand-carved, painted horses. More than 25,000 people come here every year to ride it. Even grown-ups like to climb on board.

Keep an eye out for Alice in Wonderland. You'll find her along with the Cheshire Cat, Mad

A NYC kid says:

You should definitely go to the merry-go-round and skate on Woll-man Rink at night and go to the zoo. The polar bears are really cool.

Chris, 10, New York City

Hatter, and the Dormouse at the northern end of the **Conservatory Water** (on the east side at 73rd Street) where kids and grown-ups (and Stuart Little) like to sail model boats. Look at the face of the Mad Hatter. That's actually a caricature of George Delacorte, who gave the park the statue to honor his wife. Try sliding down Alice's toadstool seat! On the west side of the water, you might be just in time for story time at the statue of Hans Christian Andersen. The statue shows Andersen reading *The Ugly Duckling,* and kids like to climb onto the book—and the duck. You can also say "hi" to Mother Goose; you'll find her sculpture at the **Rumsey Playfield** (East 71st Street), and Balto the dog (East 67th Street near the East Drive). Balto was the leader of the huskies who carried special medicine across Alaska to save people from dying of diphtheria in 1925. Bet you didn't think you were going to learn a little history here!

Math too. Keep counting. There are more than fifty fountains, monuments, and sculptures in the park.

Hungry yet? Don't worry if you forgot to bring some snacks. There are plenty of food vendors in and around the park.

If you come in the summer, you might get to go to a concert at the **Naumburg Bandshell** just south of 72nd Street in the middle of the park, or on the **Great Lawn** near the Met on the east side of the park, starting at about East 84th Street. They do rock concerts here, operas, and classical music; the New York Philharmonic even plays in the park. You can go see a puppet show at the **Swedish Cottage Marionette Theater** at West 79th Street, or row a boat. (You can get one at the **Loeb Boathouse** between 74th and 75th Streets on the east side.) There's a restaurant at the

Boathouse too. Check out www.centralparknyc.org or call (212) 310–6600 for more information.

Of course you may just want to run around, climb some rocks, or have a picnic under a tree. Where's the Frisbee?

What do you like to do best in the park? For sure the **Central Park Zoo** (at 64th Street and Fifth Avenue; www.centralparkzoo .com) will be on your list. If you're here during the holidays, you might get to see the polar bears tear open their Christmas presents. You can also go around the world at this zoo. Check out the penguins from the Antarctic Circle, bats and geckos from the rain forest, and cows and sheep that might live on American farms. There's even a roaring waterfall and tropical birds. Sometimes you can even visit the zoo's rain forest at night. Check to see if there's a program going on that allows you to help out the zookeepers. There's a great playground near the **Children's Zoo** complete

Park Hunt

While you're in the park, see if you can find:

___ Balto the Sled Dog

___ Alice in Wonderland

___ Mother Goose

___ The Carousel

___ The Dairy

___ A fancy fountain

___ A police officer on a horse

___ Strawberry Fields

___ A bridge

___ A polar bear

DID YOU KNOW?

There are 8,968 benches in Central Park. They would stretch 7 miles if placed end to end. Those benches provide a perfect place to rest and take in the park's 26,000 trees and 250 acres of lawn.

DID YOU KNOW?

Central Park is more than 150 years old. It was designed in 1853 by famous landscaper Frederick Law Olmsted. What began as 843 swampy acres is now one of the best city parks in the entire country.

DID YOU KNOW?

More than 200 movies have included scenes shot in Central Park. Can you name one? (Hints: *Men in Black II, Stuart Little, You've Got Mail, The Muppets Take Manhattan*.)

DID YOU KNOW?

There are 21 different playgrounds in Central Park and more than 200 across the city. If you go to www.centralparknyc.org and click on Virtual Park, you'll be able to view each of the Central Park playgrounds and find out exactly where they are. The Web site www.nycgovparks.org can steer you to all the city play lots.

DID YOU KNOW?

The Bronx Zoo (www.bronxzoo.com) is the largest metropolitan zoo in the country. More than 4,000 animals live here.

DID YOU KNOW?

Animals could be found in Central Park since 1858. At first, they were donated animals in an informal zoo. Today, you'll find everything from seals to sea lions to piranhas, monkeys, and polar bears.

with a 45-foot spiral slide. Don't miss the **George Delacorte Musical Clock**. It's right near the Children's Zoo at 64th Street, and every hour a nursery rhyme plays while animals glide around the base—a bear with a tambourine, a hippo with a violin, a goat with panpipes, a kangaroo with horns, and a penguin with a drum. Watch the monkeys at the top—it looks like they're hitting a ball. There's a shorter "act" on the half hour.

While the Central Park Zoo is fun, it's nothing like the huge **Bronx Zoo** at 2300 Southern Boulevard in the Bronx (718–220–5100; www.bronxzoo.com). If you like zoos, you have to get yourself on the #2 subway to the Bronx. There you can head to the African rain forest and visit more than twenty gorillas in the Congo Gorilla Forest. Maybe you'd rather meet Siberian tigers at Tiger Mountain. In the summer, you can wander amid 1,000 different kinds of butterflies and moths. Check out a black leopard in JungleWorld, an endangered snow leopard in the Himalayan Habitat, or see all the little rodents in the Mousehouse. Take the Bengali Express Monorail through Wild Asia, getting a birds-eye view of tigers, elephants, rhinos, antelope, and more.

Get ready to roll. There's a lot of ground to cover at the Bronx Zoo and you won't want to miss anything. There is a Zoo Shuttle you can take from one part of the zoo to another and a Skyfari gondola that gets you from the Asia part of the zoo to the Children's Zoo in no time.

At the Children's Zoo, which is open from April through October, you can climb into child-size heron nests, walk through a prairie dog tunnel, or climb a 20-foot spider web made of rope. In the forest, climb up a 14-foot-high platform to get face to face with a porcupine or look through a telescope. Remember to stop and feed the goats.

For more than one hundred years, this zoo has been welcoming kids and parents. It's also a center for conservation. More than 800 baby animals were born here in just one year recently! Zoo scientists travel around the world doing research to help protect endangered animals and environments.

The best part about visiting here is you'll feel like you're jumping from continent to continent, because the animals live in areas that have been designed to mimic their natural habitats, wherever in the world that may be. Besides just seeing the animals, you can also learn about how they survive—and how you can help.

Now that you've seen some exotic animals how about checking out some strange flowers and enchanting gardens? If you visit the **Botanical Gardens** (on the Bronx River Parkway at Fordham Road; 718–817–8700; www.nybg.org), you can stroll through forty-eight different gardens and see all sorts of plant life from beautiful flowers to rare and exotic trees. If it's more hands-on

activities you're looking for, visit the Botanical Gardens' new fun spot for kids: the **Everett Children's Adventure Gardens**. There are forty different activities waiting for you, including mazes, a waterfall, and even wetlands.

For wet adventures of a different kind, head down to Brooklyn. The **Coney Island Aquarium** (1208 Surf Avenue; 718–265–FISH) is home to more than 8,000 different types of animals.

If it's mermaids you're looking for, you probably won't see any at the Aquarium, but across the street at **Coney Island** (www.coneyisland.com), you just might. Known for its notorious sideshows, Coney Island sets the stage for acts beyond your wildest imagination from magicians to mermaids.

Back in Manhattan be sure to stop at the newly cleaned-up **Hudson River Park**. It would actually be hard to miss as it is a 5-mile park that is 550 acres from Battery Park to 59th Street. There's so much to do here with its skate park, batting cages, concerts, and festivals in the summer, and play areas to enjoy the snow in the winter, you won't know what to do first. Tired after all of that? No problem. Pick a tree or a nice patch of grass and take a nap. You'll feel worlds away from the actual city. And you'll understand what some New Yorkers mean when they say that New York is beautiful. To get an idea of all the rest of the things you can do here, call (212) 533–PARK or visit www.HudsonRiver Park.org.

Cyclone and More!

Ever since 1927, kids (as long as they're 54 inches tall) have headed on the subway to **Coney Island** in Brooklyn, south of Manhattan, to ride the wood-and-steel **Cyclone roller coaster,** screaming through its twelve drops, including one heart-stopping 85-foot drop. This roller coaster, with 2,640 feet of track, isn't just fun—it's a National Historic Landmark, so you can tell your parents that riding it is a history lesson! When the Cyclone opened, it was New York City's top tourism attraction. It cost a quarter then to ride (compared to $5.00 now). Experts say it's the most copied coaster anywhere in the world. Besides the Cyclone, Coney Island's **Astroland** (www.astroland.com) also has other rides, an arcade, and a kiddie park with fourteen rides. Of course, Astroland is open only in the summer. And there's always the beach. To get there, take the W subway to Stillwell Station. Exit the station and head toward the ocean. Make a left on Surf Avenue and then a right on 10th Street and you'll see the Cyclone.

CHAPTER 7

A Little Culture: Music, Dance, and Opera

Anywhere you go in the city, you are bound to find it.

Music is always in the air. It's in the parks, in the giant concert halls, on the street corners, and even down in the subway stations! You can hear anything from classical music to opera, jazz, pop, and more. It all really depends on where you head.

One of the most famous places for music in New York is **Carnegie Hall** (57th Street and Seventh Avenue). Carnegie Hall was named after businessman Andrew Carnegie. Andrew Carnegie paid for the construction of the hall back in 1890, and owned it from 1890 through 1924. Today you can hear both popular and classical music performed here. And there are many special family concerts. Have you ever heard the joke where someone visiting New York asks a man on the street how to get to Carnegie Hall? His answer: practice, practice, practice!

Famous groups from all over the world perform at Carnegie Hall. And, if you are interested in buying any music, or a musical instrument, there are a lot of music-related shops in the area. Carnegie Hall also has a weekend Family Concert series. At this series, you can learn about some of the most famous classical, jazz, and folk musicians and ensembles in America! There are hour-long performances and discussions where you can learn about how music is made or why certain instruments make certain sounds. Check the Carnegie Hall Web site at www.carnegiehall.org for details.

Going to the opera is a great way to experience cool music in New York City. I know, you probably think operas are confusing and boring because they are usually sung in different languages. But guess what? The **Metropolitan Opera Guild** offers a program called "Growing Up with Opera," where you can hear opera in a shorter and easier-to-understand English version. You'll also learn how operas are put together and you can create your own operas from scratch. Tell your teacher about the program and maybe you can have a session at your school. For more information call (212) 769–7021.

To go behind the scenes of a real opera house, visit the **Metropolitan Opera House**. If you are nine or older, you can take a backstage tour of the Met during opera season, weekdays at 3:45 P.M. and Saturdays at 10:00 A.M. On the tour, you can see sets

DID YOU KNOW?

An orchestra is a group of musicians playing instruments from four different groups—strings, woodwinds, brass, and percussion. The Strings section is made up of violins, violas, cellos, and basses. The Woodwinds are flutes, piccolos, oboes, English horns, clarinets, bass clarinets, bassoons, and contrabassoons. The Brass section is made up of trumpets, French horns, trombones, and tubas. The Percussion section is made up of snare drums, bass drums, cymbals, gongs, and auxiliaries (which are triangles or tambourines), as well as xylophones and bells. The fact that an orchestra is put together from so many different instruments is what gives it such a special sound!

DID YOU KNOW?

Music can be made from just about anything, and so can instruments. Drums can be nothing but pots and pans or plastic buckets. Organs have been made with bottles for pipes and even a soup can will make noise if you tap on it. What kind of music can you make?

DID YOU KNOW?

Throughout the city, you will see (and hear) a lot of a cappella groups. These groups don't use any musical instruments other than their voices. If you have seen a barbershop quartet on TV, you have seen an a cappella group.

DID YOU KNOW?

Washington Square Park is a hotbed for musical activity. Not only can you sit and enjoy music from local musicians, they might even let you join in! At any given time, you'll find lone guitarists to full bands jamming in the summer sun.

being created, costumes and wigs, dressing rooms, and the giant stage with its revolving platform. You need to make advance reservations so call (212) 769–7020 or visit their Web site at www.metopera.org.

The Met is located in a complex called **Lincoln Center for the Performing Arts** (www.lincolncenter.org), on the Upper West Side of Manhattan. If you take a cab to the center, tell the driver that it is between West 62nd and 65th Streets and Columbus and Amsterdam Avenues. To get there by subway, you want the #1 or #9 local train to 66th Street Station. Lincoln Center houses twenty-six different concert halls, including the Avery Fisher Hall and the New York Society for Ethical Culture.

At Lincoln Center you can find plenty of symphonies and ballets, famous musicians, and famous dancers! There is a program there called "Jazz for Young People" (in Alice Tully Hall). Through this program, you can see jazz concerts, and the performers teach you about the music. During some parts of the program, you can even take part in the music. It's usually held in November, January, and March.

If classical music is more your thing, the **Little Orchestra Society** is a program that introduces kids to orchestral music. If you have a brother or sister in preschool, there are weekend

A NYC kid says:

The best part about Central Park is all the cool shows they have there in the summer. This summer I went to see Dave Matthews, but it was too crowded. I think Lenny Kravitz played there a while back. And sometimes my parents take me to those operas on the big lawn. Those are cool because all my friends are there too.

Kelly, 14, Manhattan

73

Lollipop Concerts at the Kaye Playhouse at Hunter College. At these concerts you can learn all about classical music from four animal characters that represent each section of an orchestra. If you are older, there are also **Happy Concerts** at Avery Fisher Hall (10 Lincoln Center Plaza) at Lincoln Center, where you can experience world-famous orchestral music. For information visit www.littleorchestra.org.

The **New York Philharmonic,** the oldest symphony orchestra in the United States, performs throughout the year—around 180 concerts. When you visit, you can meet musicians from the orchestra, try out different instruments, or even make your own instrument. For more information check out www.nyphilkids.org. These concerts are held at Lincoln Center, at Avery Fisher Hall, just like the Happy Concerts. The Philharmonic performs some free concerts in Central Park every summer.

Speaking of Central Park, it offers many other summer concerts as well, and some are even free. You can see shows ranging from folk music to some of your parents old favorite singers to some of your favorite pop artists! So if you are going to be in New York in the summertime, you should check to see who is going to be playing in the park when you are there. Check out www .summerstage.com for a schedule. Maybe it will be someone you would like to see!

The **Brooklyn Academy of Music** (or BAM) (30 Lafayette Avenue; 718–636–4100; www.bam.org) is a great place to head if you are interested in hearing or learning about music from different cultures. In the springtime there is an international festival that celebrates the performing arts. At this festival you can get a great

introduction to many artists and companies from around the world. The event lasts two days, where you can see performances, workshops, and street performers and there is even a Kids' Kafe! It is an easy subway ride from Manhattan.

You can hear music wherever you are in the city, from Harlem to the South Street Seaport in lower Manhattan. In Harlem, the Big Apple Jazz Tours give you the chance to watch and maybe join in jam sessions. Call (212) 304–8186 or visit www.bigapplejazz .com. At the South Street Seaport, musicians play country and western music, bluegrass, jazz, and even sea chanteys. Lots of

The *Nutcracker* Live

Have you ever seen the *Nutcracker Suite* performed live on stage? In New York, performances of the Nutcracker are a holiday tradition at Lincoln Center. You can see the ballet at Christmas time every year, and kids from all over the city take part in it! Can you imagine playing a mouse or a candy cane on a stage at Lincoln Center? To see what other ballets are dancing into town, visit the American Ballet Theater (www.abt.org) and the NYC Ballet (www.nycballet.com).

festivals are held there, and there are always plenty of musicians playing on the street corners.

So wherever you go, music is definitely in the air. And these are absolutely some of the best places to find it.

Music in the Park

Every summer Central Park hosts a whole bunch of concerts and festivals, which go on all the way from the beginning of June through the end of August. Some of the shows are even free! If you are visiting New York in the summer time, check: www.summerstage.org. Maybe one of your favorite bands will be performing. Or you might enjoy seeing a new band you've never heard before!

Music under the Streets

If you want to hear some live music, head down to the subway stations. It may sound weird, but many great musicians enjoy playing underground, providing a little entertainment—with good acoustics— for the people waiting for their trains. You can hear singers, and people playing the guitar, the bongos, or even unique instruments—like the didgeridoo. That's an Australian instrument made out of a hollowed-out branch. There are sometimes great break dancers at the Times Square Station, too.

CHAPTER 8

Play Ball

new York City is filled with die-hard sports fans. Anywhere you go in the city, you're bound to see someone wearing a Yankees or Mets hat, a Knicks T-shirt, or a Jets or Giants jersey. You can even join in! The city has plenty of souvenir shops that sell sports paraphernalia—just pick your favorite team, and you can be a big fan too!

New York City is home to more sports teams than many cities. There are arenas, stadiums, and coliseums in Manhattan, and outside Manhattan too, where you can catch any of the teams playing or practicing. You can also watch special sporting events such as college basketball tournaments, track and field championships, professional ice-skating, and even a world-famous dog show!

If you want to see a New York sporting event, **Madison Square Garden** is a great place to go. Located on Seventh Avenue between 31st and 32nd Streets (212–465–MSG1; www.madisonsquaregarden.com), the Garden is the home of the New York Knicks basketball team (www.knicks.com), the Rangers hockey team (www.newyorkrangers.com), and the women's basketball team, the Liberty (www.nyliberty.com). The Garden also has a theater, an expo center, a "play-by-play" restaurant that has air hockey, video games, and, of course, lots of televisions with sports showing. And, the Garden also hosts lots of other events, such

A visiting kid says:

It's really exciting to go see games at Madison Square Garden, especially if the camera finds you in the audience and puts your picture up on the big-screen TV!

Melanie, 12, Connecticut

as boxing matches, circuses, wrestling, dog or horse shows, and competitive ice-skating championships.

The **Nassau Veterans Memorial Coliseum** (www.nassau coliseum.com) out in Uniondale, Long Island, is the home to the professional hockey team the New York Islanders, as well as the minor league lacrosse team, the New York Saints, and the minor league football team, the New York Dragons. Without a lot of traffic, the Coliseum should be a fifty-minute drive from Manhattan. To get there from Midtown Manhattan you want to take the Midtown Tunnel to the Long Island Expressway (495) east to exit 38, Northern State Parkway to exit 31A (Meadowbrook Parkway south) to exit M4, Nassau Coliseum. If you decide to go to the Nassau Coliseum, you definitely do not want to be wearing a Rangers jersey, because the Islanders fans will not be happy! New York sports fans are always sure that their favorite team is the very best.

Over in East Rutherford, New Jersey, is the **Meadowlands Sports Complex** (www.meadowlands.com). This sports complex is about a twenty-five-minute drive from Manhattan. A great way to get here is to head to East Rutherford, and then follow Route 120 North. Here you will find the **Continental Airlines Arena,** where big concerts are often held; **Giants Stadium;** and the **Meadowlands Racetrack.** Giants Stadium is home to the two famous New York football teams, the Giants and the Jets (though there are plans for the Jets to have a stadium of their own built in

Manhattan), as well as the professional soccer team, the Metrostars. If you're interested in horse racing, the Meadowlands Racetrack is where many of the big racing events in the area take place. Two other famous New York racetracks are **Belmont Park** and **Aqueduct,** both on Long Island. Every June, Belmont Park hosts the famous Belmont Stakes, the third leg of thoroughbred horse racing's "Triple Crown."

New York City has two great baseball stadiums, which are home to two great teams. There is **Shea Stadium,** in Flushing, Queens, which is where the New York Mets play. Shea Stadium is about twenty-five minutes away from Manhattan. It is an easy subway ride—the Willets Point stop on the #7. Or by car take the Grand Central Parkway West to the Shea Stadium exit. For more on the Mets, go to www.mets.com. There is also **Yankee Stadium,** which is in the Bronx and home to the Yankees—obviously! Probably the easiest way to reach this stadium would be by subway, because you can avoid traffic completely. Its subway stop is found right outside the stadium at the corner of 161st Street and River Avenue. You can take many different subway lines to get there, and a trip from Midtown Manhattan takes less than twenty-five minutes. The #4 train, as well as the B (weekdays only) and D trains, makes stops at 161st Street/Yankee Stadium.

If you decide you want to see a New York baseball game, you will have a great time whether you

DID YOU KNOW?

The New York Yankees have won the World Series twenty-six times and the team rosters have included such legendary players as Babe Ruth, Mickey Mantle, Roger Maris, and Lou Gehrig. Find even more information at www.yankees.com.

DID YOU KNOW?

The walkway leading into the arena at Madison Square Garden from Seventh Avenue is now known as the "Walk of Fame," and pays tribute to famous performers, athletes, announcers, and coaches. Each person honored gets a plaque that says his or her name and has a picture that represents the category that he or she is involved in (such as a picture of

a basketball, or something involving broadcasting, or even the circus). All the plaques line the walkway leading into the arena. Some of the New York athletes recognized on the "Walk of Fame" are Patrick Ewing (who played for the Knicks) and Wayne Gretzky and Mark Messier (who both played for the Rangers).

DID YOU KNOW?

The Ice Skating Rink at Rockefeller Center on Fifth Avenue and 50th Street (212–332–7654) attracts more than a quarter-million people each day from October to April. But only 150 skaters can skate at once. That's why, especially around the holidays, there are long lines to skate. You can also watch the skaters from inside the Rock Center Cafe. Sometimes people wait for a long time to get in there too. Good thing there are lots of other places around Rockefeller Center to get a snack!

choose to see the Yankees or the Mets. You will also find great food—you have to try a stadium hot dog or ice cream. Who knows, maybe you'll catch a fly ball in the stands! And, your picture may even be put up on the big-screen TV where everyone can see you! If that sounds like fun, one hint is to wear plenty of gear for the team you are seeing. Usually it's the most spirited fans that get put up on the big screen.

New York also has three minor league baseball teams. There are the Brooklyn Cyclones and the Brooklyn Kings, who both play in **KeySpan Park** (718–449–8497) on Coney Island in Brooklyn, which is around thirty minutes away from Manhattan. The easiest way to get there would probably be by subway; you just take the Q local, W, F, and N trains. Coney Island is the last stop, and all the trains stop there. When you leave the station, head toward Stillwell and Surf Avenues

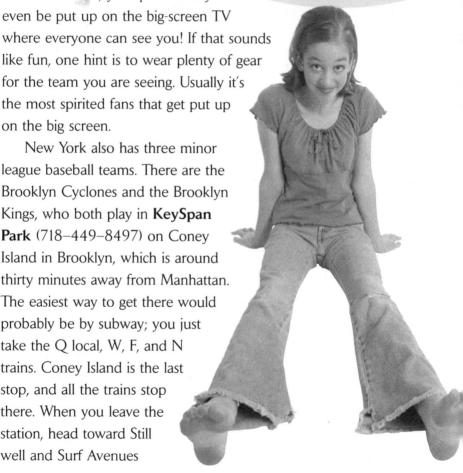

A NYC kid says:

You get a great view if you sit in the seats at the top of Yankee Stadium!

Francesca, 9, Manhattan

(walk toward Nathan's), and KeySpan Park is 2 blocks away.

Then there are the Staten Island Yankees, who play at the **Richmond County Bank Ballpark** (718–720–9265). The ballpark is about thirty minutes away from Manhattan, and the best way to get there would also be to take the subway (#4 or 5) to Bowling Green, and then take the free Staten Island Ferry. Once you get off the ferry, the park is there on your right.

Minor league baseball games can be a lot of fun and the setting is much more intimate than in the big major league stadiums. The tickets are cheaper too—usually around $8.00. You can eat plenty of great stadium food at the minor league games too, and this is the place to see baseball's rising stars.

If you feel like taking part in some of the sports yourself, New York has an amazing spot for kids—**Chelsea Piers** (www.chelsea piers.com), all the way on the West Side at 23rd Street and the Hudson River. The area is a year-round sports village. Inside, you can bowl, ice-skate at the Sky Rink, drive golf balls, slam baseballs at the batting cages, climb a wall designed specially for kids and teens, or play some basketball or soccer. If the weather's nice, there are two giant outdoor roller rinks and you can take kayak lessons. A lot of kids like to have birthday parties here. They also play in roller hockey, basketball, soccer, and lacrosse leagues. This place is so huge you won't want to leave!

Chelsea Piers is also a great place to hang out if your parents want to check out some of the "less exciting" parts of the city. Information on the **Parents' Night Out** program can be found by calling (212) 336–6500.

If you are on the Upper East Side, between First and York Avenues (1750 York Avenue to be exact), and feel like swimming in an Olympic-size pool, check out **Asphalt Green** (212–339–8890). You won't believe your eyes with all this sports complex has to offer. It's a great place to spend a few hours, but if you are going to be around for a while, try out some of the classes from chess to hip hop jazz.

Or if you want to just play out in the sun, basketball games are constantly going on at the small court on Sixth Avenue and West 4th Street. These athletes are usually pretty serious street players and definitely worth watching, but if you catch them at the right time, maybe you can get in on some action.

Or maybe it is a game of logic you are looking for. Take a walk through Washington Square Park, where on the west side you will find tables topped with chess/checker boards. You could be the next Bobby Fischer.

So, whether you're into hockey, basketball, football, baseball, or even soccer, New York is a great place to catch all the exciting games. Just choose a team and get out there and join the New York fans!

Getting Tickets to a Game

Finding tickets to a New York sporting event is not as hard as you might think—although it does depend on what game you want to see. If you want to get tickets online, www.ticketmaster.com is a good place to go, and there are many other Web sites that you can try as well. Or, you can try calling or going to the box office at the arena or stadium that is holding the event you want to see.

The New York City Marathon Has Come a Long Way . . .

The first New York City Marathon was run in 1970, and only fifty-five runners finished the race. Considering that around 30,000 athletes now compete in the marathon each year, it certainly has come a long way. The race is held every year in the fall, and many of the top distance runners from all over the world come to the city to compete. The race runs through the five boroughs of New York, starting in Staten Island, then going through Brooklyn, Queens, and the Bronx, and finishing in Central Park in Manhattan. The marathon has now become so popular that even stars like Oprah Winfrey and P. Diddy have given it a try. If you're interested in the sport of running, or just like to people-watch, the marathon is definitely an exciting event. Learn more at www.nyc marathon.org.

CHAPTER 9

Lady Liberty and Ellis Island

She was a thank-you gift from France that took more than twenty years to get here.

And when she finally did arrive, she was packed in 214 crates, like a giant jigsaw puzzle that had to be put together. Good thing they sent directions along. But what a present the **Statue of Liberty** turned out to be! Originally planned as a gift of the people of France to the people of the United States to commemorate their long friendship, she now stands in New York Harbor as the most famous symbol of liberty and freedom in the world. She's also the biggest metal statue ever constructed.

Immigrants cried when they saw her because they knew their long sea voyage was over. Today, a lot of people get choked up when they see Lady Liberty for the first time.

The original idea behind the statue was that the French people would build the statue and transport it to the United States. The Americans were supposed to build the pedestal on which she would stand. Well, the French raised the money they needed, but in the United States, no one seemed to want to give any money to help. Finally, the *New York World* newspaper launched a big campaign to raise the needed money. Even school kids contributed. People from all around the country started to send money and just before the statue arrived in 1885, enough money had been raised to build the pedestal. The statue was unveiled the next year, in October 1886.

The sculptor, Frederic Auguste Bartholdi, used his mom as the model for the Statue of Liberty's face. He spent more than twenty years on the project and put a lot of symbols into her. For example, the seven rays of her crown are supposed to represent the seven seas and the seven continents. The tablet she holds is engraved with the date of American independence, July IV, 1776, and her torch means she's lighting the way to freedom and liberty.

To get to the Statue of Liberty, you take a ferry from Battery Park across New York Harbor to **Liberty Island.** Expect very tight security! It takes about fifteen minutes and then you can take the same ferry to **Ellis Island.** You'll see the statue's original torch right in the lobby. It was replaced in 1986 when Liberty got a $100 million face-lift.

On the second floor of the Statue Pedestal, you can see replicas of the statue's face and foot. They are big! And see the work it took to create this colossal statue.

Web Sites

www.nps.gov/stli is the National Park Service Web site for the Statue of Liberty and Ellis Island.

www.ellisisland.com is the Web site for the Ellis Island Immigration Museum.

www.circlelineferry.com is the Web site for the ferry service that takes you to the Statue of Liberty and Ellis Island.

bensguide.gpo.gov is a special Web site for kids about the U.S. government.

Lady Liberty is made of copper sheets with an iron framework. It wasn't easy. The framework was designed and built by Gustave Eiffel, the great French engineer who later built the Eiffel Tower in Paris. At her feet are chains to symbolize her escaping the chains of tyranny.

Ever wonder why the statue is green? It's because the statue is made of copper, and even though this metal starts out as a brownish color, it oxidizes, or turns green, when exposed to the air. It took thirty years for the statue to turn green!

After the September 11 terrorist attacks, tourists were not allowed to climb up in the statue. But in late summer of 2004, the Statue of Liberty was reopened and visitors are now once again

Grab a Tape Measure!

The height from the foot of the Statue of Liberty to the tip of the flame is 151 feet and 1 inch. She weighs 225 tons (445,000 pounds). She's one big lady!

Index finger: 8 feet
Head: 17 feet and 3 inches
Nose: 4 feet
Right arm: 42 feet
Mouth: 3 feet wide (when she's not smiling)

DID YOU KNOW?

People in New York City come from 188 different countries and nearly half speak a second language at home. All total, kids attending New York City Public Schools speak 140 different languages.

DID YOU KNOW?

Every year, close to three million people visit the Statue of Liberty.

DID YOU KNOW?

Between 1892 and 1954, twelve million immigrants passed through Ellis Island. Before they could officially enter the United States, each one had to pass a six-second medical exam in the Great Hall to see if they had any contagious illness or disability that would keep them from being able to earn a living. Ninety-eight percent passed.

DID YOU KNOW?

When you're visiting the Statue of Liberty and Ellis Island, you're visiting a national park.

DID YOU KNOW?

You've probably heard some of these words: "Give me your tired, your poor, your huddled masses yearning to breathe free."

They're part of a very famous poem written in 1883 by Emma Lazarus. You can read the entire poem on a plaque in the museum at the Statue of Liberty.

DID YOU KNOW?

There are 354 steps from the entrance of the Statue of Liberty to the tip of her crown.

DID YOU KNOW?

You can download a special Statue of Liberty activity guide just for kids at www.nps.gov/stli/pphtml/forkids.html.

allowed to tour the statue and walk out on the observation deck. Advance reservations are required, however, so check out www.nps.gov/stili for updated information.

Ellis Island (212–363– 3200; www.ellisisland.com) is north of Liberty Island, another brief ride on the ferry. Maybe someone in your family arrived in the United States here. A lot of the immigrants were kids traveling with their parents or older brothers and sisters. The very first person to be processed on Ellis Island was a fifteen-year-old girl, Annie Moore, who was traveling with her two brothers on January 2, 1892.

Before then, individual states decided who could immigrate, but as the numbers of people coming to America increased, it got to be too big a job. **The Great Hall,** where the immigrants waited when they arrived on Ellis Island, is part of the museum. Look around. Do you think you would

A NYC kid says:

Taxis are pretty expensive in New York, so you're better off taking a bus or a subway.

Jesse, 10, New York City.

have been scared, not speaking the language, wearing clothes that looked different? Probably you would have been hungry and possibly sick after two weeks on a rocking boat.

Not everyone who came to the United States in those days came through Ellis Island—not if they had more money. First- and second-class passengers on ships didn't need to go through the process; the idea was that if they could afford a more expensive ticket, they were less likely to need the government's help in America. These immigrants only went to Ellis Island if they were sick or had legal problems. "Steerage" or third-class passengers were the ones who landed here, often after long trips on crowded ships where they faced rough seas without much chance to get any fresh air. Sometimes teens came alone, to meet an older relative.

When you visit Ellis Island, you can watch a movie about the immigrants who came here. Sometimes professional actors bring to life the stories that immigrants have told over the years—check when you arrive to see if there are any of these performances the day you visit.

You might also get to see the reenactment of an official immigrant hearing, held to determine whether someone could stay in the United States.

If you visit the **"Treasures from Home Collection,"** you can see what the immigrants brought with them. How many toys and dolls do you see? You'll see the baggage room where thousands of immigrants checked their bags while they waited to be "inspected."

If you come from a family of immigrants, you might want to

Pack Your Trunk!

When immigrants came in the last century, there was no e-mail or TV, and most people didn't have telephones. The only way to find out more about life in America was by writing a letter to a relative already here. Sometimes they exchanged photos so they'd know whom to look for when they arrived. Some teenagers came by themselves. If you were coming to America, you could only bring one small trunk containing thirty things. You can see what some immigrants chose to bring with them in the "Treasures from Home" exhibit on the third floor of the museum on Ellis Island. What would you bring?

take the chance to learn how to trace your family roots or look up a relative on the huge electronic database at the museum's **American Family Immigration History Center.** There are ships' passenger records of more than twenty-two million people from 1892 to 1924, when immigration processing was at its peak at Ellis Island. If you find your relative's name, you can get reproductions of the original lists of passengers and photos of the ships.

Make sure to stop at the **American Immigrant Wall of Honor,** just outside the "Peopling of America" exhibit. The wall is inscribed with over 600,000 names of those who came through Ellis Island. Families have paid to have their immigrant relatives'

names engraved. If you do have an ancestor listed there, you can make a pencil rubbing of the name.

When you look at all the different names from all the different countries and cultures, you can really understand why they call this country a melting pot. Your own family probably is one too. How many different countries did your ancestors come from?

Becoming a Citizen

The United States is often called a melting pot because so many immigrants have come here from different countries and cultures looking for a better life. But just living here doesn't automatically make you a citizen. If you've come to the United States from another country, to become a citizen you must:

— be at least eighteen years old.

— live in the United States for five years or more.

— be of good moral character and loyal to the United States.

— be able to read, write, and speak basic English to pass a test.

— have enough basic knowledge of U.S. government and history to pass a test.

— be willing to take an oath of allegiance to the United States.

Once you've collected all the necessary documents and passed the tests, you appear before a judge and ask to become a citizen. Then you take a special oath. It's a very exciting day. Many immigrants live in the United States their whole lives without becoming citizens.

CHAPTER 10

Ground Zero and Lower Manhattan

September 11, 2001 . . . we all remember where we were when we heard the terrible news. We watched those awful pictures again and again of the hijacked planes hitting the **World Trade Center** and the buildings collapsing from the heat of the fires. We thought a lot about kids who lost a parent or an aunt or uncle. None of us could understand why someone would do something so terrible.

The attacks changed all our lives. We realize that every time we stand in a long line to go through security at airports.

Many kids visiting New York want to go to **Ground Zero.** So do parents. You're not alone. More than 25,000 people visit every day. You'll probably see kids from around the world here with their families.

From the time they were finished, in 1976, until they were destroyed in 2001, the 110-story twin towers of the World Trade Center were the tallest buildings in New York and the anchor of the city's skyline. People used to go to the top of the World Trade Center to look out at all of New York. Now they go to the site to pay their respects. Plans for a memorial and new buildings are underway. The cornerstone for a new Freedom Tower was

Web Sites

www.renewnyc.com is a Web site that talks about the rebuilding of Lower Manhattan.

www.wtcsitememorial.org is the Web site devoted to the World Trade Center Memorial that's going to be built.

laid at the site on July 4, 2004.

There's a lot of history here as well as emotion.

When you get here, you're at the very bottom of Manhattan, the oldest part of New York City. George Washington was inaugurated near here on Wall and National Streets in 1789. Look for the **Federal Hall Memorial** (www.nps.gov/feha) that marks the spot.

Wall Street and the **New York Stock Exchange** are nearby— the financial capital of the world. The Dutch named it "Wall Street" in the 1600s because there was a wall here that marked the city limit. The New York Stock Exchange—currently closed to the public—started in 1792 when two dozen men met under a Buttonwood tree facing 68 Wall Street and started trading. Now the Exchange is the world's biggest. Stocks are shares in companies that people buy, hoping they'll make money if the company succeeds. Some stocks cost just a few dollars, but others cost a lot more. The trading area is about two-thirds the size of a football field.

The World Trade Center towers were part of a huge complex that took up 6 city blocks. About 50,000 people worked here. These days, the area looks like a gigantic construction site that's surrounded on all sides by a tall steel fence. Walk along the fence and you can read about New York City history. There's an area that's been built around the site that lets you stop and look into it.

You can watch the construction crews working with their big machines. If you come back a year from now, it will look a lot different as more of the rebuilding gets underway. In November 2003 a new PATH train station was opened in the World Trade Center site. You can take the train from Manhattan to New Jersey from here as well as see the Ground Zero construction site.

There are panels along the perimeter fence with the names of everyone who died here as well as temporary memorials. Many people bring flowers.

A lot of New Yorkers live in this part of Manhattan. Some families moved here after 9/11. Others returned as soon as they could. Many kids live and go to school in this neighborhood. The first new school built since 9/11 opened in 2003—Millennium High School. Everyone was very excited about it.

Take a look at how hard people are working to rebuild the World Trade Center site. Daniel Libeskind is the architect who designed the plan for the new World Trade Center

A visiting kid says:

I came to Ground Zero to see what it looks like now. It's good for people to come to see it so they can remember what happened on 9/11.

Joey, 11, Manchester, Connecticut

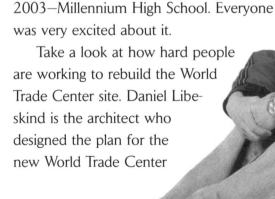

DID YOU KNOW?
In all, 2,982 people died in the attacks on September 11, 2001—2,752 died at the World Trade Center. They came from more than ninety countries.

DID YOU KNOW?
There are thirteen different museums in Lower Manhattan, from the National Museum of the American Indian to the brand-new Skyscraper Museum, and dozens of restaurants and stores. Every time you eat in a downtown restaurant, go to a museum, or buy something in a store in lower Manhattan, you're helping the recovery effort. New York says "thanks!"

DID YOU KNOW?
Nearly half the people vacationing in New York who come downtown are from outside the United States.

DID YOU KNOW?
In 1664 the city's tallest structure was a two-story windmill. Pigs roamed around Wall Street, eating the garbage and cleaning up the streets at the same time.

DID YOU KNOW?
There is now a Downtown Connection, a free bus service that runs between South Street Seaport and northern Battery Park City. You can get on and off the bus all along the way. Stops are located near key destinations throughout the neighborhood. For more information call (212) 566–6700.

DID YOU KNOW?
The vaults of the Federal Reserve Bank on Maiden Lane store more than a fourth of all the world's gold bullion.

site. Libeskind's design is called **Memory Foundations.** It will have five towers including a Memorial Garden, a museum, a performing arts center, a hotel, stores, and offices. A 1,176-foot-tall spire will create a new skyline for lower Manhattan. "We must always remember the lives of those we lost on that day," he said.

There were more than 5,000 entries from sixty-three countries to build the memorial within the sixteen-acre World Trade Center site. That's the biggest design competition in history and it's taken a long time to choose the best design. What do you think the memorial should look like?

New Yorkers and the designers hope the new buildings will show the world how strong New Yorkers are. It's going to take many years to build and when it's done, you'll still see a part of the original wall of the twin towers—a symbol of the strength of American democracy.

Kids Talk about Ground Zero

I used to live downtown. My mom came and picked me up at school and took me to my cousins. We couldn't go home. My dad worked on the fifty-sixth floor but he got out. I was really glad to see him. My brother had a play date that morning but my mother said that was no day for a play date. We couldn't go back to our house so we moved uptown. I didn't have any friends at first because I didn't know anybody in my new school, but now it's OK.

Hayley, 9, Manhattan

It's important that we always remember the people who died here.

Satesh, 9, the Bronx

My uncle was a fireman and he died on 9/11. It was very sad because so many people died.

Helen, 9, Manhattan

Ground Zero is really sad. . . . Bring a box of tissues.

Catherine, 10, Omaha, Nebraska

My mom came to pick me up at school and she was crying and I saw all the black smoke. I was really scared.

Ronni, 9, Manhattan

I like thinking about how important it was that people tried to save other people that day. It makes me feel sad, but it's good to come here with your family.

Jessie, 8, Orlando, Florida

Being here is a lot different than seeing it on TV. It makes it all much more real.

Lindsey, 14, Clinton, New York

You were lucky not to have been in New York City that day.

Jenna, 9, Manhattan

How Do You Feel?

After visiting Ground Zero, talk about your feelings with your family. What would you want NYC kids to know about how you feel?

_____

_____

_____

_____

_____

_____

_____

_____

_____

_____

_____

_____

_____

_____

_____

_____

CHAPTER 11

Where Kids Like to Eat and Shop

Grab your chopsticks and your wallet! Everyone who comes to New York loves to shop—and to eat food at restaurants that are different from home. First stop: **Chinatown,** one of New York's most unique neighborhoods. With the Chinese lanterns and telephone booths, and everyone speaking Chinese, it's like stepping into a Chinese city right in downtown New York. It's the biggest Chinatown in the United States, with more than 400 restaurants! You'll hear more Chinese spoken than English here in Chinatown, which is in Lower Manhattan just south of Canal Street and a short walk from the Lower East Side. Even the street signs are in Chinese.

If you want to learn more about the history of Chinatown and the people who settled here, stop in at the **Museum of Chinese in the Americas** (70 Mulberry Street, 2nd floor; 212–619–4785). You can browse in stores along Mott Street that sell Chinese toys, herbs, and all kinds of unusual-looking foods. But it isn't just these stores that draw the crowds—people come here to literally shop on the street. Chinatown, particularly Canal Street, is famous for its variety of street vendors who sell everything from jewelry, to handbags, to perfume. Of course you're going to eat. The restaurants here can be big or tiny. Sometimes, the waiters don't speak English, but the menus often are printed in both Chinese and English. New York kids say any kind of noodle dish is a good bet, even for picky eaters. They also like to come here on weekends for Chinese brunch called Dim Sum. You pick all kinds of little dumplings from carts the waiters roll around the restaurant. You can also find out more about Chinatown at www.chinatowninfo.com.

I love Chinatown and the Lower East Side for the knock-off Gucci purses and Tiffany jewelry, and it's really fun to bargain and get what you want for less money.

Colleen, 13, Long Island, New York

Little Italy is another old-fashioned neighborhood that's a favorite with kids and parents. It's just north of Canal Street and Chinatown. You'll find lots of little restaurants here too, where you can have pizza, pasta, lasagna, and yummy Italian pastries and ice cream. Some families like to go to Chinatown for dinner and wander over to Little Italy for dessert. If you're visiting in September, all of Mulberry Street becomes a huge outdoor restaurant at the Festival of San Gennaro.

Of course you can get any kind of food you want in New York—from an omelet in Greenwich Village to burgers in midtown to soul food in Harlem to the fanciest food you've ever seen. Some of the country's most famous chefs live and work here. You might have fun scouting out a restaurant in Greenwich Village or SoHo, where there are so many.

There are a lot of themed restaurants in New York too, including **Planet Hollywood** (1540 Broadway at 45th Street). Kids especially like the spooky **Jekyll & Hyde Club** (1409 Avenue of the Americas between 57th and 58th Streets). **Mars 2112** (1633 Broadway at 51st Street) is supposed to make you feel like you're exploring Mars. Girls like the cafe at the **American Girl Place** (609 Fifth Avenue at 49th Street) because their American Girl dolls get VIP treatment too, down to doll-size China and seats. And everyone likes the loud, funky **Ruby Foo's** (1626 Broadway at 49th Street; 212–489–5600).

Ask your hotel concierge or the people you're visiting to suggest restaurants kids like. If you go someplace fancy, go early when it won't be so crowded. Try something different that you don't eat at home. (Tip: If you're not that hungry, ask for a half portion.)

Web Sites

www.lowereastsideny.com is the Web site for the Lower East Side area of stores and restaurants.

If you're more interested in shopping than eating, there are tons of good places to go. You'll want to hit **Toys "R" Us** in Times Square and walk down Fifth Avenue.

Girls won't want to skip the new **American Girl Place** on Fifth Avenue at 49th Street, where, besides the cafe, they can even get their American Girl dolls' hair done and buy souvenirs and clothes for their dolls as well as themselves.

While you're in the neighborhood, check out the **Sony Wonder Technology Lab** (550 Madison Ave between 55th and 56th Streets; 212–833–5414; www.sonywondertechlab.com). The place is so popular you might want to make reservations. Admission is free to the four floors of hands-on video and computer games where kids (ages eight to fourteen) can do everything from test PlayStation2 games to shoot basketballs.

There are stores that sell just comic books and others kites. Ask at your hotel if you're looking for something specific.

You're bound to find a lot of what you're looking for at big New York City department stores. It seems like they've got everything! **Bloomingdale's** (59th Street and Lexington Avenue; www.bloomingdales.com) has two entire floors of kids' stuff. **Macy's Herald Square** (Broadway and 6th Street at 34th Street; www.macys.com) is still the world's biggest department store with ten floors. If you get hungry in Macy's, there's even a McDonald's in the children's department on the fourth floor!

There are lots of other stores in New York City too—big ones and small ones, stores you know like GAP, Old Navy, and H&M, and tiny spots you've never heard of. Even museums have great stores in New York. It's fun to just window shop, people-watch everywhere, and hunt for bargains.

Heading downtown, every Sunday, **Orchard Street** is closed to traffic from Delancey Street to East Houston Street, so merchants can put their wares out in the street like in the old days.

New Yorkers have always come to Orchard Street and the surrounding neighborhood looking for bargains. Today, they also come for cutting-edge fashion and great food, like dill pickles, deli sandwiches, knishes, and more. Stop in at **Katz's Delicatessen** (205 East Houston; 212–254–2246), the city's oldest. It's been dishing out pastrami sandwiches since 1888!

You'll still find great bargains on everything from leather jackets to purses to jewelry, perfume, and shoes. Don't be afraid to bargain: The store owners expect it! Stop in at the **Lower East Side Visitor Center** at 261 Broome Street, for more information about the neighborhood.

Head over to the East Village and you might notice a bit of a change in atmosphere. Walking around here can be a bit like taking a walk on the wild side. But if you are looking for the strange and unusual, you're in the right neighborhood. Vintage comics sit side by side with the most recent releases at **St. Marks Comics** (11 St. Marks Place; 212–598–9439). Speaking of vintage, at **Love Saves the Day** (119 Second Avenue at 7th Street; 212–228–3802) you can find all sorts of secondhand memorabilia from clothing to toys. Rumor has it that Madonna has been known to

donate some of her clothes to this store. Want to shock your parents? There are places all over the Village, especially on St. Marks, where you can get a henna tattoo. The art will wash off in just a few days—but your parents don't have to know that! At **Trash & Vaudeville** (4 St. Marks Place; 212–982–3590) you can try on a pair of platform boots or maybe even some crazy snake earrings.

Don't forget your birthday money!

Dancing (and Shopping) in the Streets

In the summer, the city comes alive like at no other time. Not only are there more people outside just enjoying the nice weather, there are festivals and fairs all over the place. At any given time in the warmer months, you will very likely find a street fair. In fact, you'll probably walk right into one. Here's a list of some that are particularly geared toward kids, but for a complete listing, check out www.nycstreetfairs.com.

Earth Day Awareness Festival (April)
Waverly Place from Broadway to Fifth Avenue

Children of the World Festival (May)
Avenue of the Americas from 42nd to 56th Streets

52 Association Jazz Festival (June)
52nd Street from Lexington to Seventh Avenue

The Summer Seaport Festival (July)
Water Street from Fulton to Broad Streets

Manhattan Youth Fair (August)
Murray Street from Broadway to Church Streets

MECA (Multi-Cultural Education and Counseling through the Arts) Family Festival (around Labor Day)
Third Avenue from 34th to 42nd Streets

Avenue of the Americas Family Expo (October)
Avenue of the Americas from 42nd to 56th Streets

Lullaby of Broadway Festival (November)
Broadway from Fulton to Battery Place

Not Just Meat and Potatoes

Hungry? Think of a food, no matter how bizarre, and you can probably find it—and maybe even a restaurant dedicated totally to it—in the city. Sink your teeth into these:

Peanut Butter & Co.
240 Sullivan Street
(212) 677-3995
http://ilovepeanutbutter.com
With twenty-one different ways to eat peanut butter here, the name of the Web site says it all.

Chat n' Chew
470 Sixth Avenue
(212) 243-8226
Everyone always says not to talk with your mouth full, but it will be hard to keep your mouth shut about how great the huge portions of comfort food are here.

Cowgirl Hall of Fame
519 Hudson Street
(212) 633–1133

After a long day on the range, all cowboys and cowgirls like to hoot it up with some good chow. So relax, pardner and come in for some grub.

Grilled Cheese
168 Ludlow Street
(212) 982–6600

Come on, what else do we need to say??!!

A visiting kid says:

If you want the best candy shop ever and some pretty good ice cream, too, go to Dylan's Candy Bar across the street from Bloomingdale's at Third Avenue and 60th Street.

Rae, 13, Connecticut

Vendor Alert

You'll see them all over the city. Street vendors sell everything from CDs, DVDs, books, hats, scarves, jewelry, watches, sunglasses, and much more. Many sell their own artwork around the museums. Maybe a photo or watercolor would make a good souvenir. Just be skeptical if a vendor tells you they've got the hottest brands. Chances are you're getting a "deal" because they're offering you a knock-off, not the real thing. Don't buy anything without bargaining.

Food Smarts

A lot of kids who come to New York City try food they haven't eaten at home. Check off what you've tried:

___ A hot dog from a street vendor

___ A hot salted pretzel or roasted nuts from a street vendor

___ A slice of pizza folded in half (that's the way New Yorkers eat it)

___ A pastrami sandwich

___ A fresh bagel with a schmear (of cream cheese)

___ Chinatown noodles or rice with chopsticks

Write down something you ate in New York that you hadn't tried before:

_____

_____

Macy's Thanksgiving Day Parade

The first floats were pulled by horses, and live animals—even camels and elephants—were part of that first Macy's Christmas Day Parade, which was held on Thanksgiving Day in 1924.

Today, of course, people around the world watch the parade on TV. More than 2.5 million parents and kids line the route from Central Park West at 70th Street down Broadway to 34th Street

Did You Know?

Bloomingdale's (1000 Third Avenue at 59th Street, 212–705–2000) was founded in the late 1800s on the Lower East side by two brothers, Joseph and Lyman Bloomingdale, selling hoop skirts. They moved uptown to Lexington Avenue and 59th Street in 1886. That's where you'll still find the big department store. The store created its own nickname in 1973 when it stamped "Bloomies" on panties for a promotion.

Did You Know?

The average New York City taxi travels 64,000 miles a year. All told, an estimated 650,000 people ride in New York's cabs each day. There are 12,187 licensed taxicabs in New York.

Did You Know?

There are 8,453 subway cars and 4,930 buses in New York. Nearly eight million people ride the city's subways and buses each day. You pay your fare by swiping a MetroCard that you can buy at a subway station. Up to three children 44 inches tall and under can ride for free when accompanied by a fare-paying adult. Don't lose your card!

Did You Know?

The arrival of Santa has been the grand finale of the Macy's Thanksgiving Day Parade every year except in 1933. That year he got to ride at the head of the parade! He "lives" at Macy's Santaland (West 34th Street at Herald Square) after the parade until Christmas Eve. More than 300,000 kids come to visit him at the gigantic Santaland, which also has talking trees, caroling bears, friendly elves, and spinning lollipops. Get there early or be prepared to wait. The lines to meet Santa can get very long.

near Macy's. There are bands—they compete from all over the country to get a spot—clowns, floats, singers, dancers (including the Radio City Rockettes), and, of course, the giant balloons.

The balloons have been a parade tradition since 1927. In fact Macy's uses more helium to blow up its giant balloons each year than anyone else in the country, except the U.S. government. A team of ten artists works on designing and building the balloons all year long. A lot of New York kids like to watch the balloons being inflated the night before the parade. This is a pretty eerie sight. The balloons are rolled out and anchored with sandbags to keep them from flying away. (Hint: If you're there the night before, wander around West 77th to 81st Streets between Columbus and Central Park West between 3:00 and 10:00 P.M.) The balloon line-up takes up 2 full city blocks! Go to www.macys.com to learn more about the parade.

Don't Forget . . .

Your favorite NYC restaurant:

_____

What did you eat there?

_____

Your favorite NYC store:

_____

What did you buy there?

_____

CHAPTER 12

What a Trip!

You had such a great time in New York; you don't want to forget any of it.

You can draw some pictures and paste in some photos too.

Here's Where I Stayed:

I came to New York City with

_____

_____

_____

_____

It was

___ hot

___ raining

___ cold

___ snowing

On my favorite day in New York, I

went to _____

ate at

bought _____

I saw

on Broadway.

It was great because _____

_____

I saw these famous New York City sites:

___ The Empire State Building

___ Times Square

___ The skyline from the Circle Line boat

___ The Statue of Liberty

___ Ellis Island

Every book has its list of top sites. Here's your chance to make your own: Write down your top picks from the places you've been in New York.

1.

2._____

3.

4._____

5.

The best meal I had in New York was

_____

My favorite NYC souvenir is

_____

My best New York memory is

_____

Appendix

General Web Sites

www.nycvisit.com

www.nyc.gov

Attractions

American Immigrant Wall of Honor, Ellis Island, 212–561–4500; www.wallofhonor.com

Astroland at Coney Island, 1000 Surf Avenue Brooklyn; 718–265–2100; www.astroland.com

Big Apple Circus, Damrosch Park; Lincoln Center at 62nd Street; 800–922–3772; www.bigapplecircus.org

Botanical Gardens, on the Bronx River Parkway at Fordham Road; 718–817–8700; www.nybg.org

Brooklyn Academy of Music, 30 Lafayette Avenue, Brooklyn; 718–636–4100; www.bam.org

Bronx Zoo, 2300 Southern Boulevard, Bronx; 718–220–5100; www.bronxzoo.com

Carnegie Hall, 57th Street and Seventh Avenue; 212–903–9600; www.carnegiehall.org

Central Park, www.centralparknyc.org

Central Park Zoo, at 64th Street and Fifth Avenue; 212–439–6500; www.centralpark zoo.com

Chelsea Piers, 17th to 23rd Streets along the Hudson River; 212–336–6666; www.chelsea piers.com

Chrysler Building, 405 Lexington Avenue at 42nd Street

Circle Line Tour, Pier 83, West 42nd Street; 212-563-3200; www.circleline.com

Coney Island, 1208 Surf Avenue in Brooklyn; 718–372–5159; www.coneyisland.com

Coney Island Aquarium, 1208 Surf Avenue in Brooklyn; 718–265–FISH

Donnell Library Center, 20 West 53rd Street; 212–621–0618; www.nypl.org

Ellis Island, 212–363–3200; www.ellisisland.com; www.nps.gov/elis

Empire State Building, 350 Fifth Avenue between 33rd and 34th Streets; 212–736–3100; www.esbnyc.com

Federal Hall Memorial, 26 Wall Street; 212–825–6888; www.nps.gov/feha

Grand Central Terminal, 42nd Street at Park Avenue, 212–340–2210; www.grandcentral terminal.com

Ground Zero, www.renewny.com, www.wtcsitememorial.org

Hudson River Park, Battery Park to 59th Street; 212–533–PARK; www.HudsonRiverPark.org

Lincoln Center for the Performing Arts, 1941 Broadway at 65th Street; 212–546–2656; www.lincolncenter.org

Madame Tussaud's New York Wax Museum, 234 West 42nd Street, 800-246-8872; www.nycwax.com

Metropolitan Opera House, between Columbus and Amsterdam Avenues and West 62nd and 65th Streets; 212–362–6000; www.metopera.org

Mid-Manhattan Library, 445 Fifth Avenue at 40th Street; 212–340–0833; www.nypl.org

MTV Studios, Broadway between 44th and 45th Streets; www.mtv.com

NBC Studios, www.shopnbc.com

New York Stock Exchange, www.nyse.com (currently closed to the public)

Ringling Brothers and Barnum & Bailey Circus, www.ringling.com

Rockefeller Center, Fifth to Seventh Avenues, 47th to 51st Streets, 212–332–6868; www.rockefellercenter.com

Sony Wonder Technology Lab, 550 Madison Avenue between 55th and 56th Streets; 212–833–5414; www.sony wondertechlab.com

South Street Seaport, 207 Front Street; 212–732–8257; www.southseaport.org

Statue of Liberty, Liberty Island; 212–363–3200; www.nps.gov/stli

United Nations Building, First Avenue between 42nd and 48th Streets, with public entrance at 46th Street; 212–963–4440; www.un.org

Wollman Rink, East side of Central Park between 62nd and 63rd Streets; www.wollmanskatingrink.com

Museums

American Museum of Natural History, 175-208 Central Park West at 79th Street, 212–769–5000; www.amnh.org and www.ology.amnh.org

Brooklyn Children's Museum, 145 Brooklyn Avenue, 718–735–4400; www.brooklyn kids.org

Children's Museum of the Arts, 72 Spring Street; 212–941–9198; www.cmany.org

Children's Museum of Manhattan, 212 West 83rd Street; 212–721–1234; www.cmom .org

Cloisters, Fort Tryon Park at 193rd Street; 212–923–3700; www.metmuseum.org

El Museo del Barrio, 1230 Fifth Avenue at 104th Street; 212–831– 7272; www.elmuseo.org

Ellis Island, 212–363–3206; www.ellis island.com

Guggenheim Museum, 1071 Fifth Avenue at 89th Street; 212–423–3500; www .guggenheim.org

Intrepid Sea-Air-Space Museum, Pier 86 at 12th Avenue and 46th Street; 212–245–0072; www.intrepidmuseum.org

Lower East Side Tenement Museum, 90 Orchard Street; 212–431–0233; www .tenement.org

Madame Tussaud's New York Wax Museum, 234 West 42nd Street, 800–246–8872; www.nywax.com

Metropolitan Museum of Art, Fifth Avenue and 82nd Street; 212–535–7710; www .metmuseum.org

Museum of American Folk Art, 45 West 53rd Street; 212–265–1040; www.folkartmuseum.org

Museum of Chinese in the Americas, 70 Mulberry Street; 212–619–4785; www.moca-nyc.org

Museum of Modern Art, 212–708–9400; www.moma.org

Museum of Television and Radio, 25 West 52nd Street; 212–621–6600; www.mtr.org

New York City Fire Museum, 278 Spring Street; 212–691–1303; www.nycfire museum.org

South Street Seaport Museum, 207 Front Street; 212–748–8600; www.southseaport .com

Restaurants
Ben's Kosher Deli, 209 West 38th Street at Seventh Avenue; 212–398–2367

Cafe Un Deux Trois, 123 West 44th Street at Sixth Avenue; 212–354–4148

Carmine's, 200 West 44th between Broadway and Eighth Avenue; 212–221–3800

Chat n' Chew, 470 Sixth Avenue; 212–243–8226

Cowgirl Hall of Fame, 519 Hudson Street; 212–633–1133

Dylan's Candy Bar, at 60th Street and Third Avenue; 212–620–2704

Ellen's Stardust Diner, 1650 Broadway at 51st Street; 212–956–5151

ESPN Zone, 1472 Broadway at 42nd Street, 212–921–3776; http://espnzone.com

Grilled Cheese, 168 Ludlow Street; 212–982–6600

Jekyll & Hyde Club, 1409 Avenue of the Americas between 57th and 58th Streets; 212–541–9505

Katz's Delicatessen, 205 East Houston Street; 212–254–2246

Mars 2112, 1633 Broadway at 51st Street; 212–582–2112

Ollie's Noodle Shop and Grill, 190 West 44th Street, 212–921–5988

Peanut Butter & Co., 240 Sullivan Street; 212–677–3995

Planet Hollywood, 1540 Broadway at 45th Street; 212–840–8326

Ruby Foo's, 1626 Broadway at 49th Street; 212–489–5600

Tavern on the Green, West side of Central Park; between 66th and 67th Streets; 212–873–3200; www.tavernonthegreen.com

Virgil's Real BBQ, 152 West 44th Street off Broadway; 212–921–9494

Shopping

American Girl Place, 609 Fifth Avenue at 49th Street; 877–AGPLACE; www.americangirl.com

Bloomingdale's, 100 Third Avenue at 59th Street; 212–705–2000; www.bloomingdales.com

CBGB Records, 315 Bowery; www.cbgb.com/records.htm

Lord & Taylor, 424 Fifth Avenue at 39th Street; 212–391–3344

Love Saves the Day, 119 Second Avenue at 7th Street; 212–228–3802

Macy's, 151 West 34th Street; 212–695–4400; www.macys.com

St. Marks Comics, 11 St. Marks Place; 212–598–9439

Saks Fifth Avenue, 611 Fifth Avenue at 50th Street; 212–753–4000; www.saks.com

Toys "R" Us, (1514 Broadway at West 44th Street; 800–869–7787; toysrustimessquare.com

Trash & Vaudeville, 4 St. Marks Place; 212–982–3590

Virgin Megastore Times Square, 1540 Broadway at West 45th Street; 212–921–1020 www.virginmegastore.com

Sports Facilities

Aqueduct Race Track, 110-00 Rockaway Boulevard, Jamaica, Long Island; 718–641–4700; http://www1.nyra.com/aqueduct

Asphalt Green, 1750 York Avenue; 212–339–8890

Belmont Park Race Track, 2150 Hemstead Turnpike, Elmont, Long Island; 516–488–6000; www.nyra.com/Belmont

Chelsea Piers, 17th to 23rd Streets along the Hudson River; 212–336–6200; www.chelseapiers.com

KeySpan Park, Coney Island, 1904 Surf Avenue, Brooklyn; 718–449–8497; www.brooklyncyclones.net/mainpark.shtml

Madison Square Garden, Seventh Avenue between 31st and 32nd Streets; 212–465–MSG1; www.madisonsquaregarden.com

Meadowlands Sports Complex, East Rutherford, New Jersey; 201–935–8500; www.meadowlands.com

Nassau Veterans Memorial Coliseum, 1255 Hempstead Turnpike, Uniondale, Long Island; 516–794–9303; www.nassaucoliseum.com

Richmond County Bank Ballpark at St. George, 75 Richmond Terrace, Staten Island; 718–720–YANKS; www.siyanks.com

Shea Stadium, 123-01 Roosevelt Avenue, Flushing, Queens; 718–507–METS; www.mets.com

Wollman Rink, East side of Central Park between 62nd and 63rd Streets; www.wollmanskatingrink.com

Yankee Stadium, 161st Street and River Avenue, Bronx; 718–293–4300; www.yankees.com

Theater

Apollo Theater, 253 West 125th Street; 212–531–5300; www.apollotheater.com

Brooklyn Academy of Music, 30 Lafayette Avenue in Brooklyn; 718–636–4100; www.bam.org

Dance Theater of Harlem, 466 West 152nd Street; 212–690–2800; www.dancetheater ofharlem.com

Disney's New Amsterdam Theater, 214 West 42nd Street; 212–282–2900; www.disney.go.com/DisneyTheatrical/New Amsterdam/

Happy Concerts, www.littleorchestra.org

Lincoln Center for the Performing Arts, 1941 Broadway at 65th Street; 212–546–2656; www.lincolncenter.org

Metropolitan Opera House, between Columbus and Amsterdam Avenues and West 62nd and 65th Streets; 212–362–6000; www.metopera.org

New Victory Theater, 42nd Street, west of Broadway; 212–239–6200; www.newvictory.org

Radio City Music Hall, 1260 Avenue of the Americas, at 50th Street and Sixth Avenue; 212–247–4777; www.radiocity.com

Swedish Cottage Marionette Theater, Central Park, west side at 79th Street; 212–988–9093; www.centralparknyc.org /virtualpark/thegreatlawn/swedishcottage

TKTS, 47th Street and Broadway or South Street Seaport, at the corner of Front and John Streets; www.tdf.org

Tourism

Lower East Side Visitor Center, 261 Broome Street; 212–226–9010

Times Square Visitors Center, 1560 Broadway between 46th and 47th Streets; 212–869–5667; www.timessquarebid.org